Anonymous

Talks with Socrates about Life

Translations from the Gorgias and the Republic of Plato

Anonymous

Talks with Socrates about Life
Translations from the Gorgias and the Republic of Plato

ISBN/EAN: 9783337189433

Printed in Europe, USA, Canada, Australia, Japan

Cover: Foto ©ninafisch / pixelio.de

More available books at **www.hansebooks.com**

TALKS WITH SOCRATES

ABOUT LIFE

TRANSLATIONS

FROM

THE GORGIAS AND THE REPUBLIC

OF

PLATO

NEW YORK
CHARLES SCRIBNER'S SONS
1887

PREFACE.

The dialogue which occupies the larger part of this volume, although generally known by the name of the rhetorician Gorgias, sometimes bears the sub-title of *Rhetoric*. This latter may seem a strange designation for a work the aim of which is nothing less than to discover wherein happiness, or, what to Plato is a synonymous term, The Good, consists. But, as his great master had brought down philosophy from the "world of pure thought" to the daily haunts of men, — to the street, the market-place, the public Assembly; so Plato deemed no subject so trivial that its relation to The Good might not profitably be ascertained, none so remote that it might not form a connecting link between men's daily lives and the universal object which "every soul pursues, and for the sake of which it does all that it does."[1] Surely, then, the art which was more persistently and systematically cultivated than any other by the Athenians of the time of Socrates and Plato is no inappropriate heading to this search after "the best way of life."

Chief among the causes contributing to the popularity of rhetoric or, as it has been defined, "the power of discerning every possible means of persuasion upon every subject"[2] was the recent establishment of dikasteries or courts of justice, in which large numbers of the citizens

---

[1] Republic, 505 E. [2] Aristotle, Rhet. i. 2, p. 1355 b 26.

were compelled to sit daily as jurymen. The necessity which was thus laid upon every Athenian to take an active interest in questions of law, and still more the innate love of litigation which rendered a summons before a tribunal a matter of frequent occurrence, naturally predisposed the public mind to listen with favour to teachers who promised to impart " the faculty of persuading judges in the courts of justice by means of words." It is no mere figure of speech that Callicles uses when he tauntingly asserts that, if unprovided with the weapons of defence afforded by rhetoric, the accused " would stand there with swimming head and open mouth, and with never a word to say; nay, would have to die if his accuser, however mean and low he were, chose that death should be the penalty."

Our information concerning the scope and nature of the art, one of whose most famous representatives we are about to meet, is chiefly derived from our knowledge of the sophists, with whom, Plato tells us, the rhetoricians were commonly identified. The very closeness of the relationship between rhetorician and sophist would seem, it is true, only to have enhanced the contempt in which each held the other. Callicles, for instance, though figuring here as the host and admirer of Gorgias, speaks of the sophists " as men of no account whatever;" while the rhetorician Isocrates heaps upon them even fiercer invectives than those contained in the pages of Plato, their arch-enemy, as he is called by Grote. Nor were the sophists more measured in the contempt they expressed for the art which, taking no cognizance either of theory or principle, confined itself to one narrow aim, that of persuasion. Nevertheless, sophist and rhetorician were commonly held to be " the same person considered under a different point of view," and as such we shall for the present regard them.

What, then, do we know of the teachers whose name has become a very synonym for specious reasoning, and to define whom, as Plato himself tells us, "involves great hardship and a dangerous chase"?[1] The name itself must not be thought of as applicable to any distinct school of philosophy or system of thought. Grote, who may be regarded as the chief rehabilitator and champion of the sophists, calls them the "practical teachers of Athens," and declares that unless we take into account all the existing circumstances "we cannot fairly estimate them face to face with their accuser-general, Plato. He was a great and systematic theorist.... Their direct business was with ethical precept, not with ethical theory; all that was required of them, as to the latter, was that their theory should be sufficiently sound to lead to such practical precepts as were accounted virtuous by the most estimable society *in Athens*. It ought never to be forgotten that those who taught for active life were bound, by the very conditions of their profession, to adapt themselves to the place and the society as it stood."[2]

That the sophists were mere exponents of the average morality of the day is, however, one of the chief charges which Plato brings against them. He complains that instead of leading they only echo the opinions of the multitude. He compares them to the man who, adapting himself to the humour of some wild beast whom it is his duty to feed, has no notion of good and evil save from the fancies of the animal;[3] he describes them as mercenary hunters of the young and wealthy, as traffickers of the wares pertaining to the soul;[4] and casts

---

[1] Sophist, 218 D. [2] Grote's Greece, vol. viii. chap. 67.
[3] Republic, 493 A. [4] Sophist, 231 D.

ridicule upon them as champions of the art of contention in words; as members of the money-making tribe of the art Eristic, which he calls the art disputatious, controversial, pugnacious, and contentious.[1] And although the evidence of so prejudiced a witness as Plato ought not to be received as conclusive, it may not unfairly be assumed that he does to some extent reflect the public opinion of his time. The blush, therefore, which it costs the young Hippocrates to declare his intention of joining the ranks of the sophists;[2] the half defiant tone with which Protagoras proclaims his readiness to throw off the mask hitherto worn by his predecessors and proclaim himself the sophist that he is;[3] the assertion that they who are most powerful and esteemed are ashamed to write speeches because they fear that in after-times they may be called sophists;[4] all this would seem to indicate that, although the fiend called "die Sophistik" dressed up, as Grote declares, by recent German historians, may be set down as purely a creature of the imagination, the most prominent teachers of the day had nevertheless come to be regarded with suspicion if not distrust by at least a portion of the community.

The above allusion to the sophists as a "money-making tribe" may be regarded as significant of the difference that existed between them and those who were steadfastly "looking onward to the Truth." It is not easy for us to conceive of the repugnance with which thoughtful men of that day regarded the association of emolument with positions of honour and trust. If the recent innovation of paying the servants of the state, such as the dikasts and soldiery, had excited a storm of opposition, what must have been the feeling aroused on beholding

---

[1] Sophist, 231 E;.226 A.
[2] Protagoras, 312 A.
[3] Ibid., 317 B.
[4] Phaedrus, 257 D.

what was regarded as the highest of human relationships — that existing between teacher and pupil — affected by questions of pecuniary gain! It has been well said that "the distinction between the sophists' sale of knowledge for money and the free conversation of Socrates with all comers may not seem much in itself, but it is a type of the profound difference in the moral purpose of Socrates on the one hand, and of Protagoras, Gorgias, and Hippias on the other. To say that the sophists represented the average morality of Greece is not a defence; it is a condemnation. Those who come before the world as wise men and teachers ought to have something more than average morality to offer." [1]

If, therefore, Plato's view may be accepted, that the office of teacher is to educate and nurture the soul; to gently draw it from out the barbaric slough in which it has long lain buried, and lead it to look upward;[2] to turn it from the shadowy illusions of sense to the Idea of Good which is the dispenser of truth and reason, and to point out the best way of life, it is plain that rhetoric was still more unfitted than sophistry for this high function. The one, at least in theory, recognised the necessity for a knowledge of principles, whereas it was the boast of the other that its faculty of assuming the appearance of every other art did away with any such necessity, thus proving conclusively that the one and only unmistakable reality is the power of humbug. "I have heard, dear Socrates," says Phaedrus, "that he who wishes to be a rhetorician has no need to learn what is the true nature of justice, but only what it appears to the crowd who sit in judgment; nor what is the good and the

---

[1] "Grote's Plato" in Sat. Review, July 22, 1865.
[2] Republic, 533 D.

noble, but only what appears thus; for of this, not of Truth, is persuasion begotten."[1] As we read these words we cannot but feel that they only too well describe certain standards of our own day. Indeed, throughout the whole dialogue it is constantly brought home to us that, although the palmy days of oratory are over and a public of listeners has, with us, in great measure given place to one of readers, although, as Carlyle asserts, "the Journalists are now the true Kings and Clergy," there are still statesmen and teachers whose personal magnetism and fluent speech serve to screen corrupt principles and ignoble aims. Theirs is the oratory of which Plato says that it is mere flattery and base clap-trap, used by pseudo-statesmen to gratify the humours of the populace, and to coax it into such blind compliance with their own will as shall enable them with impunity to abuse public trusts for purposes of private gain.[2] Such was the estimation in which Plato held the teachers whose promise to implant knowledge within the soul, "as if they would put sight into blind eyes," is perhaps no unfit gauge of their own criterion of wisdom.

Widely removed, however, from the counterfeit art here so scathingly denounced is the true one, concerning which we are told that "without much hard work it can never be acquired, but must nevertheless be cultivated for the sake of speaking and acting, to please not men but God, and in all things to do, so far as may be, his pleasure."[3] It is to this "true art of rhetoric" that Socrates refers when he calls himself the only Athenian who practises statesmanship with a view not to gratify his fellow-citizens, but to change the bent of their desires, knowing well that unless he can implant virtue within

[1] Phaedrus, 260 A. [2] Gorgias, 502 E. [3] Phaedrus, 273 E.

their souls he can give them no other good gift. Small wonder that men of this stamp, who are themselves freed from the delusions of sense, and who behold the realities of which the ignorant perceive only the shadows, have no desire to descend into the arena of public life. Small wonder that they would fain dwell in the "world of pure thought" did not a stern sense of duty compel them to bear their share in the toils of the state, and thus help men in the upward journey towards the Idea of Good typified by "the sun, the lord of light." It is because the myth of the Cave,[1] whence this simile is taken, so beautifully depicts the combat in which they must engage who would have "the eye of the soul turned to the light," and because it so uncompromisingly points out the duty devolving upon the best-endowed natures not to stand aloof from the struggle out of which they themselves have come victorious, that it has been given a place in the present volume as a fit conclusion to a search after "the best way of life."

It is time, however, that we turn from the subject-matter of our dialogue to the men who take part in it. In several of Plato's works the main dialogue is introduced by a shorter one, in the same way that in the opening scene of a modern comedy some subordinate character puts us at once into relation with the action and the chief personages. But in the present instance we are left to our own unaided conjectures as to time, place, and circumstances. From the absence of greetings between the belated guests and the already assembled company, among whom Gorgias is the chief figure, it is a matter of doubt whether these have already taken place before the opening remarks of Callicles, or whether we

[1] See p. 121.

are to suppose some break in the dialogue during which they occur. The character of these remarks, however, forbidding, as it does, the possibility of their having been made within hearing of Gorgias, lends weight to the latter hypothesis. Whether the scene of action is to be thought of as in the house of Callicles or in some well-known place of public resort is open to conjecture. There are obstacles in the way of either supposition, but they are perhaps best reconciled by imagining that Callicles, coming by chance to the door of his house at the same moment that Socrates and his friend appear before it, holds a short conversation with them while he leads them into the presence of Gorgias, at which juncture the break would occur during which the greetings proper to the occasion are exchanged.

Whatever the place of assemblage may have been, the audience which had been summoned by Gorgias to his "delectable feast" was evidently a large and enthusiastic one, to whose encouraging and untiring applause is perhaps due the continuation of the discussion at a moment when it seemed in danger of being abandoned. The eager group which at break of day Socrates and his friend Hippocrates found clustered round Protagoras[1] is matched by the no less enthusiastic listeners who, long after Gorgias has ended his previous oration, linger on the scene lest perchance they lose some word of wisdom which may fall from his lips. Their attitude of unquestioning acquiescence is revealed by the complacent remark of Gorgias that it is a long time since any one has asked him anything new. Had these same listeners known what was now to be offered them in place of the rhetorical display which a short time before had held their

[1] Protag. 315 A.

delighted attention; had they foreseen that the art which, they would fain believe, combined all other arts within itself, was to be proved as stupid and useless as it was immoral, and the power it assured its followers shown to be a mere semblance of power capable of affording only a semblance of pleasure, — they would perhaps have looked forward with less eagerness to the coming discussion; nay, they might even have exclaimed with Callicles that, if all this were true, this life of theirs was completely upside down, and they had all their lives been doing the very opposite of what they ought.

Those already familiar with the famous Protagoras, whose portrait is given in the dialogue bearing his name, may find it interesting to compare that noted sophist with this the most celebrated of the rhetoricians, whose oratorical gifts, displayed on various embassies from his own city of Leontini, had won him a reputation throughout Greece. Both may be taken as fair examples of the literary lions of the day, whom select Athenian coteries delighted to honour. The precise claims which these teachers put forth vary, of course, with their respective professions. Sophistry does not confine itself to mere technical skill in speech, or even to that "judgment whereby a man becomes master of his own private affairs and of those of the public as well,"[1] but includes the acquisition of virtue; rhetoric, on the other hand, substitutes intellectual and moral qualities for the empty show of them which its own ingenuity affords.

As the two men resemble one another in the vastness of their pretensions, so do they in their self-importance and assumption of superiority. It is easy to recognise in Gorgias the man who, as the story goes, delighted to

[1] Protag. 318 E.

array himself in robes of purple and gold, and who caused a golden statue to be erected in his own honour at Delphi. Were it not for his childlike ingenuousness, his self-commendatory remarks, when contrasted with his inability to defend his own position against the attack of Socrates, might challenge a harsher judgment than is awarded him. But it is only with amused interest that we hear him exclaim, in answer to the question whether he is to be called a rhetorician, "Ay, and a good one, too!" and mark the complacency with which, when his brevity of speech has called forth the applause of Socrates, he observes, "I really think I am fairly good at this." And we note, with an indulgent smile, the amiable egotism and love of approbation, so skilfully played upon by the well-timed encouragement and encomiums of Socrates as to justify the subsequent reproach of Callicles that Gorgias was shamed into saying what was counter to his real beliefs out of deference to the general opinion of mankind. In truth, some such motive as this can alone have prompted the assent of Gorgias to the intimation of Socrates that the rhetorician must both know and teach moral truths; for the opposite proposition, that "the rhetorician has nothing to do with truth,"[1] accords far better with his celebrated assertion, that "nothing exists; or if it does we cannot know that it does; or if we did, we could not convey the knowledge thereof to others."

But whatever may be his convictions or want of convictions, the *manner* of Gorgias is invariably characterised by a courtesy and good-breeding which contrast favourably with the behaviour of Protagoras under somewhat similar circumstances.[2] Although he has just ended a

[1] Phaedrus, 272 E. [2] Protag. 334-9; 348; 360.

fatiguing discourse, he betrays no impatience or reluctance on being urged to repeat it for the benefit of his belated hearers. The cheerful serenity with which he meets the officious intrusion of Polus is no less remarkable than is his willing consent again to take up the interrupted conversation. His wish might well have been not to continue an argument in which he must have foreseen that he would be worsted; nevertheless, as in honour bound, he does not shrink from carrying out to the letter his promise of talking with any one who desires. When at last he is fairly reduced to silence, far from maintaining a sulky dignity, he not only continues to follow the argument with unabated interest, but, even when the conclusion bids fair to be no pleasing or flattering one, he urges Socrates not to refrain on his account from saying all that is in his mind.

The unfailing deference and courtesy which marks the conduct of Socrates towards the excellent Gorgias is in striking contrast with his rough handling of Polus, his second opponent, whose inflated style of speech he does not hesitate to parody to his face. He makes no secret of his desire to exclude him from the conversation,— a vain attempt in view of the hopeless obtuseness with which Polus seizes every occasion to thrust himself into prominence. The logical inconsequence of this "coltish" disciple of Gorgias is well illustrated by his remark when told that rhetoric is a counterfeit branch of the art of politics. "Well, what then," he inquires, "do you mean that it is a fine thing or a base one?"— an observation which calls forth the first and only discourteous speech recorded of Gorgias, who straightway bids Socrates let Polus alone, and make clear to *him* the definition which the other had not the wit even to recognise.

It is plain that, although himself the author of a pretentious essay, Polus has never used his own mind, but has merely adopted the catch-words of the school of shrewd self-interest to which he belongs. The contemptuous incredulity with which he hears that pleasure is not the highest good betokens his incapacity to grasp an idea so opposed to the standards of this school; and only because he is unable to maintain the contrary against the resistless logic of Socrates does he finally acknowledge that the gratification of ignoble and selfish desires is not the most honourable of standards. From assured self-complacency he passes to petulant impatience, from scornful derision to peevish exasperation, until he finally subsides into a condition of bewildered acquiescence, and, with the remark that "these are strange sayings," drops out of the conversation and is heard of no more.

His withdrawal gives an opening to Callicles, whom we may imagine to have been with difficulty restrained from bursting in upon the conversation, like Thrasymachus in the Republic, with whom, indeed, he has more than one point of resemblance. Although the superior in wealth, position, and family, as well as in intellectual calibre, of the pretentious bully whose only weapon is invective, he is on the same plane with him in point of unscrupulousness and unfairness. Having begun by asserting his superiority to his predecessors on the score of tenacity of opinion, he is not to be driven from his position by any proofs, however convincing. If forced into an unwilling concession, he pretends that he has made it out of pure condescension. Repeatedly does he attempt to divert the argument by accusing Socrates of ranting, of hair-splitting, or of wilfully misunderstanding him; and when he is at last fairly driven to the wall, he turns the tables upon his opponent by pretending all along to have meant what only the latter's dulness had failed to apprehend. For one moment, it is true, he seems to waver, nay, to be on the point of returning to his first vague premonitions that he *may* all his life have been believing the reverse of what he ought, that the truth *may* lie beyond the narrow horizon which embraces all his ken. But the "love of Demus" has too fast a hold upon him. We leave him with the declaration upon his lips that to be the flatterer of the State is better than to be its benefactor, and with the conviction strong within him that morality is only a set of rules which inferior men have contrived to impose upon those who are by the law of nature their masters.

Last upon our list of characters is Chaerephon, known as one of the exiles from Athens during the rule of the Thirty, and also from the mention of him (in Charmides) as a "kind of madman,"[1] an epithet probably derived from the peculiar excitability of his temperament. He it is whose enthusiastic admiration of Socrates prompted the visit of inquiry to the shrine of Delphi, which resulted in the oracle that "none was wiser than Socrates." A far from flattering description of his personal appearance is given by Aristophanes, who speaks of his "pale face and slovenly attire," and nicknames him, from the blackness of his eyebrows, "the Bat." The part played by Chaerephon in this conversation is important only because his solicitations have occasioned the delay which leads to the conversation before us.

In the Socrates of this dialogue there are traces of the almost reckless humour which is remarkable in the

[1] See also Apology, 21 A.

Protagoras. We recognise in him the prototype of what Carlyle calls the "ironic man, who, with his sly stillness and ambuscading ways, more especially an ironic young man, from whom it is least expected, may be viewed as a pest to society. Have we not seen persons of weight and name coming forward, with gentlest indifference, to tread such a one out of sight, as an insignificancy and worm, start ceiling high (*balkenhoch*) and thence fall shattered and supine, to be borne home on shutters, not without indignation, when he proved electric and a torpedo!" We behold here the "pitiless disputant, whose dreadful logic was always leisurely and sportive; so careless and ignorant as to disarm the wariest and draw them in the pleasantest manner into horrible doubts and confusion. . . . No escape; he drives them to terrible choices by his dilemmas, and tosses the Hippiases and Gorgiases with their grand reputations, as a boy tosses his balls. The tyrannous realist!—Meno has discoursed a thousand times at length on virtue before many companies, and very well, as it appeared to him; but at this moment he cannot tell what it is,—this cramp-fish of a Socrates has so bewitched him."[1]

It has been conjectured that Plato wrote these pages under stress of the intense feeling aroused by the recent trial and death of Socrates, and that his object was to vindicate his master's fame, as well as to warn those who had wrought the deed that a far more formidable trial-scene awaited them. Nobler vindication there could hardly be than the words which seem to sum up the life of Socrates: "Bidding farewell to those things which most men count honours, and looking onward to the

[1] Emerson, Representative Men.

Truth, I shall earnestly endeavour to grow so far as may be in goodness, and thus live, and thus, when the time comes, die."

But, probable as is the conjecture that the desire to vindicate his master was Plato's chief inspiration, the subject itself suffices to explain the deep current of earnestness which runs through the whole dialogue and betrays itself now and again in a passionate outburst of feeling. The theme he has chosen deals with questions "of no slight import, but those which it is perhaps the noblest thing in the world rightly to understand;" the conflict which he depicts is the old yet ever new warfare waged between the worlds of the Material and the Ideal; the one denying the existence of moral law, and refusing to see in standards of right and wrong anything beyond mere expediency and convention; the other resting its faith upon that high instinct (or may it not be more fitly called inspiration) which urges a man to be afraid not of death but of wrong-doing, and points out to him "the way of right-living," by walking in which each "may best live the time he has yet to live" and so pass through the great combat of life that after death he may "present his soul whole and undefiled."

CONTENTS.

	PAGE
GORGIAS	1
THE REPUBLIC	121
NOTES	135

GORGIAS.

GORGIAS.

CHARACTERS OF THE DIALOGUE.

GORGIAS *of Leontini, a rhetorician.*
POLUS, *a disciple of Gorgias.*
CALLICLES, *an Athenian man of the world.*
SOCRATES.
CHAEREPHON, *a friend of Socrates.*

The scene is laid either in the house of CALLICLES, *or in place of meeting.*

GORGIAS.

Callicles. A fit time this, Socrates, so they tell us, to come in for fight and fray![1]

Socrates. What! Have we, as the saying goes, arrived the day after the feast and missed it?

C. And a delectable feast it was too; for only just now Gorgias was giving us many choice specimens of his art.

S. Well, Callicles, it is all the fault of Chaerephon here; he would keep us lingering in the market-place.

Chaerephon. Never mind, Socrates, I will make amends as well. Gorgias, you must know, is a friend of mine, so that he will give us another exhibition, at once if you like, or some other time if you prefer it.

C. What is this, Chaerephon? Is Socrates eager to hear Gorgias?

Ch. To be sure; that is just what we are here for.

C. Why then, you have only to come to my house; for Gorgias is staying with me, and will give an exhibition for you there.

S. A good suggestion, Callicles. But would he care to converse with us, do you think? What I want is to find out at first hand exactly what the man's art amounts to, and what it is that he professes and teaches. As to the rest of his exhibition, he can, as you say, give that some other time.

C. Nothing like asking the man himself, Socrates! And, indeed, this was one part of his exhibition; for just now he requested that any of those present should ask him whatever questions they liked, and promised that he would answer all.

S. That is capital. Do you, Chaerephon, ask him.

Ch. What am I to ask?

S. What he is.

Ch. How do you mean?

S. Why, suppose he had happened to be a maker of shoes by profession, he would have answered you, I suppose, that he was a cobbler. Do you not understand what I mean?

Ch. I understand, and will ask him.[2] Tell me, Gorgias, is Callicles here right when he says that you give out you will answer whatever question any one may ask you?

G. Quite right, Chaerephon. That is just what I gave out a moment ago, and I may add that in these many years no one has ever asked me anything new.

Ch. Then, of course, Gorgias, it will be easy enough for you to answer.

G. You can make trial of this, Chaerephon, if you like.

Polus. To be sure; but upon me, Chaerephon, if you please, for Gorgias seems to me quite tired out. He has just got through a long discourse, you know.

Ch. What, Polus! Do you suppose you could answer better than Gorgias?

P. And what has that to do with it, if I answer well enough for you?

Ch. Nothing; pray answer, if you wish to do so.

P. Ask then.

Ch. Very well, I will. Suppose Gorgias had happened to be an adept in the art professed by his brother Herodicus,[3] what would it have been proper for us to call him? Just what we call his brother, would it not?

P. Of course.

Ch. Then, if we had called him a physician, we should have spoken correctly.

P. Yes.

Ch. And if he had been an adept in the art of Aristophon, the son of Aglaophon,[4] or his brother, what would it have been right to call him?

P. A painter, to be sure.

Ch. Well then, in what art is he an adept, and by what name therefore would it be right to call him?

P. Many, Chaerephon, are the arts belonging to mankind which have been discovered experimentally from experiences! for experience makes this life of ours to go on by system, inexperience by chance.[5] Now in each one of these arts men severally in several ways bear their several parts; in the best arts the best men, of whom Gorgias here is one, and he has to do with the noblest of arts.

S. So far as speech-making goes, Gorgias, Polus seems right well primed, but he certainly is not doing what he promised Chaerephon.

G. How do you mean, Socrates?

S. So far as I can see, he has not answered the question.

G. Well then, question him yourself, if you like.

S. No, not if you yourself are willing to answer. Nay, I had much rather it were you; for, from the way Polus has been talking, I am quite sure that he has paid more attention to what goes by the name of rhetoric than to the art of dialectics.[6]

P. How so, Socrates? *how come*

S. Because, Polus, when Chaerephon asks you in what art Gorgias is an adept, you fall to praising the art, just as if some one were finding fault with it; but you do not answer what it is.

P. Why, did I not answer that it was the noblest one of all?

S. To be sure you did. But then no one

was asking the nature of the art of Gorgias, but only what name it bears and what Gorgias himself ought to be called. Just as a while ago, when Chaerephon was putting his questions, you answered him with such admirable brevity, so do you now answer and tell us what the art is and what we are to call Gorgias. Or, rather, Gorgias, do you tell us yourself what we are to call you: what art is it that you profess to be master of?

G. The art of rhetoric, Socrates.

S. So we are to call you a rhetorician, are we?

G. And a good one, too, Socrates; that is, if you wish to call me what, as Homer says, "I boast myself to be."[7]

S. Certainly I do.

G. Call me this then.

S. And we are to say, are we not, that you are able to make rhetoricians out of other men also?

G. That at least is what I profess, not only in this place, but elsewhere as well.

S. And would you be willing, Gorgias, to go on just as we are doing at present, now questioning, now answering, and to put off to some other time that diffuse style of talking which Polus started? Come, do not belie your promise, but consent to answer my questions briefly.

G. There are some answers, Socrates, which

must of necessity be given at length. Not, however, but that I shall do my best to be brief; for this is another of my claims, that no man can say any given thing more briefly than myself.

S. Just what we want, Gorgias! Pray give us a specimen of this same brief style; the diffuse one we will have some other time.

G. I will do so with pleasure, and you shall confess that you have never heard any one speak more briefly.

S. Come then! You profess to be an adept in the art of rhetoric, and to be able to make rhetoricians of other men. Now what are the things with which rhetoric has to do? As weaving, for instance, has to do with the making of garments, — has it not?

G. Yes.

S. And music, has not that to do with the composition of melodies?

G. Yes.

S. By Hera, Gorgias, I admire your answers. You certainly are answering in the fewest possible words.

G. I really think, Socrates, that I am fairly good at this.

S. And you are quite right. Come then, answer in the same way about rhetoric, and tell me what that is of which rhetoric is the science.

G. Language.

[449 E – 452 D   Socrates here asks to be informed why every other art as well may not be styled "rhetoric," inasmuch as every art, gymnastics, for instance, in treating of the body's condition, or medicine, in prescribing remedies, necessarily employs the medium of language.

"Because," replies Gorgias, "while other arts depend upon manual skill of some kind, rhetoric has to do with language exclusively."

"I fear," remarks Socrates, "that I do not quite understand how you mean to classify it, but I dare say I shall have a clearer notion by and by."

He then points out that while in some arts, such as painting and sculpture, language plays but a small part, others there are, such as arithmetic and geometry, which, no less than rhetoric, are almost entirely dependent upon language; insomuch that one disposed to be contentious might trip Gorgias up here, by exclaiming, "And so, Gorgias, you call arithmetic rhetoric, do you?"

It appears, therefore, that only by ascertaining the object for which it uses language can the true definition of rhetoric be reached; and what that object, or, in other words, what the subject matter of rhetoric is, its great champion is now called upon to declare.

Gorgias is ready with his answer: —

"The greatest of human concerns, Socrates, and the best."

"But here, too," Socrates objects, "your statement is a questionable one, and not as yet clear. At many a banquet you must have heard that old drinking song[8] wherein health is ranked as the greatest treasure, next, beauty, and third, well-gotten riches.[9] Now they who produce these three things — namely, the physician, the trainer, and the money-maker — may be supposed to urge each his claim. 'Socrates,' the physician will say, 'Gorgias is deceiving you; not his art, but mine it is which has to do with the greatest good of man; for what, I ask you, is there greater than health?' And the trainer, in his turn, thus: "I too, Socrates, should be amazed if Gorgias could show a greater good to be derived from his art than I from mine, the end whereof is beauty and physical strength.' And after him the money-maker, with lofty superiority, I suspect, to all the rest, would come and say: 'Consider well, Socrates, whether it seems to you possible that either Gorgias or any other man should deem any treasure superior to wealth?' And were you to maintain that your own art did bring about some greater good, the assertion would only bring upon you another question. Which question Socrates now proceeds to ask:—]

S. Come now, Gorgias, imagine yourself to be questioned by these men as well as by myself, and answer us what this thing is which you call man's greatest blessing, and in which you claim to be a master-workman?

G. A thing, Socrates, which is in very truth the greatest blessing, and which gives men freedom for themselves, and at the same time mastery over other men, each in his own city.

S. And what, pray, do you call this thing?

G. I call it the faculty of persuading, by means of words, judges in the courts of justice, and senators in the Senate, and citizens in the Assembly or any other meeting of a political nature. I tell you that by means of this power you shall have as slave the physician, and as slave the trainer; nay, the very money-maker shall be seen making money not for himself but for another, — for you, namely, who have power to speak and win over the multitudes.

S. Now, indeed, Gorgias, you have, I think, made it as plain as possible what kind of art you take rhetoric to be. You maintain, if I at all understand you, that rhetoric is the creator of persuasion; that persuading, in fact, is its whole business, and that in this its crowning aim is fulfilled. Or can you maintain that rhetoric has power to do more than work persuasion in the souls of the listeners?

G. By no means, Socrates; to me this definition of yours is quite satisfactory, for its crowning aim is just this.

S. Listen then, Gorgias, to me. For you

may rest assured that if ever one man talked with another from a desire to get at the very heart of the question discussed, I — at least so I flatter myself — am one of that sort, and so I believe are you.

G. Well, Socrates, what next?

S. I will tell you presently. In regard to this persuasion which comes from rhetoric — just what you mean by it, and about what things it is persuasive — I am, you must know, not quite certain; although I confess I am not without a suspicion as to what you understand by it, and what the things themselves must be. But none the less shall I ask you what you do understand by the persuasion which comes from oratory, and what the things are to which it applies. But why, you may ask, when I have my own suspicion, should I question you at all, and not rather speak out myself? It is not out of consideration for you, but in order to help the argument and make it take such a course as will give us most light upon the subject we are discussing.

[453 C – 455 D Socrates justifies his present mode of procedure by arguing that just as upon hearing Zeuxis [10] spoken of as *the* figure-painter we should forthwith inquire wherein his figures differ from those of other figure-painters, so now, knowing that many arts besides rhetoric have to do with persuasion, it no less behooves us to discover the nature of the persuasion wrought by rhetoric. To which Gorgias promptly replies, that he refers to the persuasion exercised in the law courts as to what is just and what is unjust. This answer, however, does not touch the real point at issue, and Socrates now approaches it from another side.

"Do you take knowledge and belief," he inquires, "to be one and the same thing? Surely not. For, were one to ask you,—'Are there, Gorgias, such things as false belief and true belief?' your answer would undoubtedly be in the affirmative; whereas false knowledge, as all men know, is an impossibility. And yet they who have come to know and they who have come to believe are alike persuaded! Persuasion, then, is of two kinds, the one working belief, the other knowledge; and that produced by rhetoric is clearly of the former kind, since it were manifestly impossible in the short space allotted to a session of the Assembly to impart any real knowledge upon such a subject as the just and the unjust. Indeed, that such is the generally received opinion is seen from the fact that whenever choice has to be made of state physicians or generals or ship-builders, or master craftsmen of any kind, or whenever walls are to be built or harbours to be constructed, it is not the rhetorician, but the man most skilled in the art or profession in question, who is called upon for advice."

"But what," says Socrates in conclusion, "does Gorgias himself think about these matters? For it is just that we should learn of them from one who not only calls himself a rhetorician, but is able to make rhetoricians of other men; and all the more since there are those among the audience who, though anxious to become his pupils, are ashamed to ask questions for themselves. Let Gorgias, then, imagine himself to be confronted, in the person of Socrates, by the whole company when he is asked the question, 'And what, Gorgias, shall we gain by becoming pupils of yours? On what civic affairs will you render us capable of offering advice? Only those which concern justice and injustice, or those mentioned by Socrates as well?'"

To this appeal Gorgias makes the following reply:—]

G. I will certainly do my best, Socrates, to make clearly known to you the whole scope of oratory; in fact you yourself have given me an excellent suggestion how I may do so. You are aware, I suppose, that the dockyards in question, and the walls of which the Athenians boast, and the construction of the harbours were due chiefly to the advice of Themistocles, partly also to that of Pericles, but not at all to that of the master craftsmen.

S. So it is commonly said, Gorgias, as regards Themistocles; and as to Pericles, I myself heard him when he advised us about the Middle Wall.[11]

456 *G.* And whenever a choice, Socrates, has to be made in the matters you have spoken of, it is, as you see yourself, the rhetoricians who advise, and whose judgment, moreover, prevails.

S. Yes, Gorgias, and it is because I wondered at all this that I asked a good while ago what the art of oratory really amounts to. For when I look at it in this way, its extent seems to me something marvellous.

G. Ah, but if you only knew everything about it, Socrates, — how it gathers up, as it were, and contains all the other arts in itself! And of this I can give you a striking proof. Often before now I have been with my brother or with other physicians to visit some patient of theirs who refused either to take their medicine or to submit to operation, whether by the knife or by cautery; and when the physician could find no way of persuading him, I have prevailed upon him solely by this art of rhetoric. And I maintain that were a rhetorician and a physician to go together into any city you choose, and there, either in the Assembly or in some other public meeting, discuss the question which of the two should be elected physician, the physician would show for nothing, while he who had the gift of speech would carry the election if he had a mind to it.[12] And if he were to enter into a contest with any expert whomsoever, the rhetorician could persuade people, far better than the other, into electing him; for there is no subject upon which the rhetorician could not speak more persuasively before the multitude than could any expert whosoever. Such, then, is the scope, and such the nature of the art. Nevertheless, Socrates, we must use rhetoric just like skill in any other exercise. For in other exercises no one man has a right to turn his strength against every other man just because he has so mastered the art of boxing and wrestling and using arms as to have both friend and foe at a disadvantage; that is no reason why he should strike and stab his friends, — aye, and slay them too. Neither, by Zeus, if a man, who from frequenting the palaestra[13] has got his body into good fighting condition, were to strike his father or mother or any other of his kinsfolk or friends, would it be right on account of this to hate the trainers and those who teach the art of fighting in armour, and banish them from our cities. For they gave their teaching that it might be rightly used in self-defence against the enemy and the wrong-doer, not in assault; but these other men pervert their strength and their art, and put them to improper use. Not that the teachers are bad, nor is the art itself bad or to blame for all this; but they are to blame who do not use it properly. Now the same thing applies to rhetoric. True enough, the rhetorician has the power to hold his own against all men and upon all subjects, so as to have more influence than others with the multitude on any subject that he may choose. But none the more for this—that he *could* do it—has he the right to take away the credit either of the physician or of any other expert. No, indeed; he ought to use his rhetoric fairly, just as he does skill in other exercises. And it seems to me that if, after becoming a rhetorician, he puts this power and the art itself to an unjust use, it is not the teacher who ought to be hated and banished from the city. For he imparted the art to be used for justice, but the other uses it contrariwise. Wherefore the man who misuses it is the one to be hated and cast out and put to death, not he who taught it.

S. I suppose, Gorgias, that you, like myself, have had much experience in discussions, and have noticed this peculiarity of them, that the disputants do not find it easy to define for each other's benefit the subjects they may have undertaken to discuss, and thus to bring the conversation to an end, feeling that they have mutually received and imparted knowledge. Instead of this, if they happen to be at issue upon a certain point and the one says that the other speaks incorrectly or obscurely, they get angry, and each imagines that the other is speaking out of jealousy, in a spirit of disputation,[14] not seeking out the gist of the matter. And some there are who end by bringing things to a most disgraceful pass, reviling and calling one another such names that those present are vexed with themselves that they ever thought such men worth listening to. Do you ask why I say all this? Because it strikes me that what you now say does not agree or harmonize very well with what you said at first about rhetoric. But I am afraid to refute you, lest you suspect me of talking, not out of eagerness to have the matter made clear, but out of spite to you. Now, if you are a man of the same sort as myself, I should much like to cross-question you; if not, I should prefer to let you alone. Of what sort am I, do you ask? One of those glad to be refuted if I say what is not true, and glad to refute another if he should say what is not true; and no less glad, I assure you, to be refuted than to refute, since this I believe to be a greater good in just the same degree that it is a greater good to be set free one's self from the greatest evil than to set another free. For I believe that there is no evil so great for a man as to hold false opinions upon the questions with which our argument has to do. If this, therefore, is the sort of man you call yourself, we will go on talking. But if you think best to break off here, we will do so forthwith, and make an end of the discussion.

G. On the contrary, Socrates, I too claim to be a man of the sort you describe. I suppose, however, we ought to bear in mind the wishes of the company. For, a while ago, before you came in, I had been discoursing to them at some length; and if we carry on the discussion now, we shall very likely prolong it unduly. We must, therefore, consider their wishes, lest we detain them from some thing else they may want to be doing.

Ch. The applause of your audience, Gorgias and Socrates, which you hear for yourselves, shows how eager they are to listen to whatever you may have to say; and for my own part, Heaven forbid that I should ever be in such want of leisure as to give up a discussion of this kind, and upon such a subject, because something else was more pressing.

C. True, by the gods, Chaerephon! Why, even I myself, although of course I have been present at many a discussion ere now, doubt if I was ever so delighted before; so that, if you will only consent to go on talking all day long, I for my part shall take it as a favour.

S. I assure you, Callicles, that, so far as I am concerned, there is nothing to prevent, if only Gorgias will consent.

G. After all this, Socrates, it would be a disgrace for me not to consent, especially after I myself have given out that I will answer whatever any one wishes to ask. Pray, then, if the company so desire, open the discussion and ask whatever question you please.

[458 E – 460 E   Courteously imputing a certain inconsistency in the statements of Gorgias, to which attention is to be called, to some misapprehension on his own part, Socrates first asks whether he would really maintain that the rhetorician need be conversant with no art whatever, since he can always persuade the ignorant that he himself knows more than any expert. "Yes, Socrates," Gorgias replies, "and is it not a great saving of trouble, if, after learning this one art and no other, a man may find himself at no disadvantage compared with those who have mastered other arts?"

With the remark that the question of advantage or disadvantage will more properly come in at another stage of the argument, Socrates proceeds to inquire, whether this assertion respecting the arts may be held to be true of moral qualities as well, or whether a man must on the contrary acquire a knowledge of justice and injustice before he can become a rhetorician. The latter alternative is accepted by Gorgias, who does not attempt to gainsay the deduction immediately drawn from it, that just as the man who has learned music has become a musician and he who has studied medicine a physician, so he who has learned justice has become a just man and as such is incapable of acting unjustly.[15] This too ready compliance on the part of Gorgias enables his opponent to prove the inconsistency above alluded to, which he proceeds to do as follows : —]

S. From what you said on the subject, I supposed at the time that rhetoric, which is forever discoursing of justice, could not possibly itself be an unjust thing; so that, when you stated a little while afterwards that the rhetorician might possibly use his art unjustly, I was struck with amazement, and, thinking
461 that the two statements did not chime together, made the remark that if, like myself, you held it a gain to be refuted, it was worth while to go on with our discussion ; if not, it would be better to give it up. But having come since then to look into the matter anew, we are now agreed, as you yourself see, that the rhetorician is incapable of using his art unjustly or being willing to commit injustice. By the dog,[16] Gorgias, it will take no little talking to investigate all this thoroughly.

P. What, Socrates, do you really believe that all you are now saying about rhetoric is true ? Do you not rather suppose that Gorgias was ashamed not to grant you that the rhetorician must needs have a knowledge of the just and the beautiful and the good, and that if any one comes to him lacking this knowledge he himself will impart it; and that it is perhaps in consequence of this admission of his that some little contradictions have occurred? But you, of course, are delighted, having yourself led us into this kind of questioning. Why, who do you suppose would ever deny that he understands justice himself and is ready to impart it to others? But it is very ill-mannered of you to lead up to a discussion of this kind at all.

S. Nay, but, Polus, my good friend, we get for ourselves friends and children on purpose that, when we grow older and make missteps, you younger ones may be at hand to set us again in the right course, as to both words and deeds. So now, if Gorgias and myself are making any misstep in our argument, do you, pray, be at hand to set us right again; for this you are bound to do. And if it seems to you that any one of these admissions has not been properly made, I am ready to let you take back whichever you please, if you will only do me the favour to be careful about one thing.

P. And what is that?

S. To keep within bounds, Polus, the long-winded style which you undertook to use at first.

P. What! Am I not at liberty to say as much as I please?

S. Truly, my excellent friend, you would be badly off indeed if you had come to Athens,

where in all Greece there is greatest liberty of speech, and there found that you were the only man to fail of it. But just reverse matters. Suppose you go on talking at length and refusing to answer questions, should not I in my turn
462 be badly off unless I were at liberty to go away and not listen to you? Nay, if you care anything at all for the argument in which we have been engaged, and wish to have it set straight again, take back, as I said before, whatever you see fit; and then in your turn, like Gorgias and myself, proceed to question and answer, and so refute or be refuted. For I suppose you profess the same art with Gorgias, do you not?

P. I do.

S. Do you, too, then, make the request that any one at any time will ask you any question he likes, seeing that you know how to answer?

P. Yes, to be sure.

S. Then do now whichever of the two you prefer, — question or answer.

P. Very well, I will; and do you, Socrates, answer me. Since you think that Gorgias is at a loss how to define rhetoric, tell us yourself what it is.

S. Are you asking me what art I take it to be?

P. I am.

S. No art at all, Polus, in my opinion, if I must tell you the truth.

P. What, then, do you take rhetoric to be?

S. A thing which, as you maintain in the treatise of yours which I was reading lately, has created art.

P. What do you understand by it?

S. In my opinion it is a kind of dexterity.

P. What! you look upon rhetoric as a matter of dexterity![17]

S. I do, unless you have another name for it.

P. Dexterity in what?

S. In the production of a certain gratification and pleasure.

P. Well, if rhetoric is able to gratify men, do you not think it a fine thing?

S. How is this, Polus? Have you already found out from me what I call it, that you go on to ask whether I do not think it a fine thing?

P. Have I not found out that you call it a kind of dexterity?

S. Tell me, since you prize affording gratification so highly, are you willing to gratify me in a mere trifle?

P. Certainly.

S. Ask me, pray, what sort of an art I take fancy cookery to be.

P. Well, I ask you, what sort of an art is fancy cookery?

S. No art at all, Polus.

P. What is it, then? Pray tell us.

S. Yes, I will tell you; a kind of dexterity.

P. In what? Tell me that.

S. Certainly I will. In the production of gratification and pleasure.

P. Fancy cookery, then, and rhetoric are the same, are they?

S. Oh, no, indeed; but branches of the same pursuit.

P. Of what pursuit do you mean?

S. I am afraid it may be somewhat discourteous to declare the truth; in fact, I hesitate to speak on account of Gorgias, lest he imagine that I am turning his own pursuit into ridicule. For my part I really do not know whether or not this is the rhetoric which Gorgias practises, as what was said just now has not shown us clearly what he thinks about it; but the thing I call rhetoric is a branch of something which certainly cannot be styled "fine."

G. What is it, Socrates? Pray speak out, and do not let me embarrass you.

S. Well then, Gorgias, I look upon it as a pursuit which has nothing to do with art, but requires merely a bold, shrewd mind, clever at getting on with men; and the sum total of it I call flattery.[18] Of this pursuit there are, I hold, many branches besides, one of these being fancy cookery, which bears indeed the semblance of an art, but in my opinion is no art at all, but a mere matter of dexterity and routine. Rhetoric, too, I call a branch of the same, and likewise personal adornment and sophistry,— these four branches corresponding to four classes of actual things. Now if Polus wishes to find out my opinion, let him set about it at once; for as yet he has not found out which branch of flattery I pronounce rhetoric to be, but, without noticing that I have not yet given him an answer, he goes on to ask if I do not think it a fine thing. But I shall not tell him whether I look upon rhetoric as a fine thing or a base one, until I have first answered what it is; for that, Polus, would not be right. No; if you wish to find out my opinion, you must ask me which branch of flattery I pronounce rhetoric to be.

P. Very well; I ask now, and do you answer, — which branch is it?

S. Will you know any better, I wonder, after I have answered? For, in my opinion, rhetoric is a counterfeit of a branch of the political art.[19]

P. Well, what then? Do you mean that it is a fine thing, or a base one?

S. To my mind, a base one. For bad things I call base, since I am to answer you with the understanding that you already know what I mean.

G. By Zeus, Socrates, I really do not myself understand what you mean.

S. Very likely, Gorgias, for I have not as yet made my point clear; but Polus here is so young and coltish.[20]

G. Well, let him alone, and tell me what

you mean by saying that rhetoric is the counterfeit of a branch of the political art.

S. Very well, I will try to tell you what rhetoric seems to me to be; and if it is not as I say, Polus here shall refute me.

[464 A – 465 E   Gorgias readily admits that a right condition, whether of body or of soul, may be so skilfully counterfeited as to deceive any save an expert. Such a result flattery contrives to bring about in the following manner. The art called political, which provides for the soul's interests, and the art which has charge of the body, have each alike two divisions, consisting in the latter case of gymnastics and medicine, in the former of legislation and justice. Now, flattery, being, as aforesaid, no art at all, cares not a whit for the welfare of either soul or body. But, though devoid of any knowledge of principles, and though aiming solely at bringing foolish men under her spell through the bait of pleasure, she has the shrewdness to assume the likeness of the arts above-mentioned. So successfully, for instance, does fancy cookery, one branch of flattery, feign a knowledge of the food best for the body, that were the fancy cook and the physician to present themselves for election before a tribunal of boys, or men as foolish as boys, the physician, for all the encouragement he would receive, might die of want; and each of the other arts has in like manner its own counterfeit. Thus, to state the thing mathematically, as personal adornment is to gymnastics so is sophistry to legislation, and as fancy cookery is to medicine so is rhetoric to justice.

Here Socrates pauses to point out that, although the relative positions of rhetoric and sophistry are in reality such as he has asserted, yet so closely related are the two that they are very commonly confounded even by those who profess them.[21] Taking up the simile again, he declares that had the body, not the soul, been deputed to judge upon all questions of food and medicine, and had our sole standard been one of mere bodily delight, the saying of Anaxagoras would undoubtedly long since have come to pass, and all things relating to medicine, health and cookery would ere now have become entangled in one indistinguishable and inextricable mass.[22] He then closes with the following apology:—]

S. And now, I dare say I have been inconsistent, in that, while I would not allow you to talk at length, I myself have made a long speech. However, I deserve to be excused, inasmuch as when I spoke in few words you were unable to understand, nor were you able to make anything out of the answer I gave you, but you needed to have it explained. If I,

therefore, in my turn can make nothing out of
466 your answers, you in your turn must speak at
length; but if I can, you must let me, for this
is only fair. So now if you can make anything
out of the answer in question, pray do so.

P. Well, what is it you say? That you
look upon rhetoric as the same with flattery?

S. I said it was a *branch* of flattery. But
how is it, Polus, that at your age you do not remember? What will you do by and by?

P. You think then, do you, that in our
cities the good rhetoricians, being regarded as
flatterers, are held in low esteem?

S. Is this a question you are asking, or is it
a beginning of a speech?

P. A question, to be sure.

S. They are not esteemed at all; at least,
so it seems to me.

P. How not esteemed? Is it not they who
are most powerful in our cities?

S. Not if you call power a good thing for
the man who possesses it.

P. Most certainly I call it so.

S. Then to my mind, of all men in the community, the rhetoricians have least power.

P. What! Is it not true of them, as of the
tyrants,[23] that they can put to death any man
they please, or rob him of his possessions, or
turn him out of our cities, if they see fit?

S. By the dog, Polus, with every statement
you make, I am in doubt whether you are

speaking for yourself and setting forth your own opinions, or whether you are asking me a question.

P. I am asking you a question, of course.

S. Very good, my friend. But why do you ask me two questions together?

P. How two?

S. Did you not say something just now to the effect that the rhetoricians, like the tyrants, put to death any man they please, or rob him of his possessions, or drive him out of our cities, if they see fit?

P. I did.

S. Well, I tell you that these are two questions, both of which I shall answer you. First of all, Polus, I maintain, as I said just now, that the rhetoricians and the tyrants have the least possible power in the community, for they do nothing, so to speak, that they would, though they do, to be sure, whatever they think best.

P. And is not this having great power?

S. No; at least, so says Polus.

P. I say no? I say yes, I tell you.

S. Not you, by ——,[24] since you maintain that great power is a good thing for him who has it.

P. Of course I maintain it.

S. And do you look upon it as a good thing, if a man who has no sense may do whatever suits his own pleasure; and do you call this having great power?

P. No, I do not.

S. Prove to me, then, that the rhetoricians
467 are men of sense, and that rhetoric is an art,
not a flattery, and you will have refuted me.
But if you let me go unrefuted, it will then
appear that this is no good thing which is possessed by the rhetoricians, those who do whatever they please in our cities, and by the tyrants; that is, if power, as you maintain, is a
good thing, and doing what one pleases, without understanding, an evil one, as you admit it
is, — do you not?

P. I do.

S. How, then, could rhetoricians or tyrants
possibly have great power in our cities, unless,
indeed, Socrates were to be refuted by Polus
and made to confess that they do what they
would?

P. This fellow —

S. I deny that they do what they would;
now refute me, if you can.

P. Have you not just admitted that they do
what they think best?

S. Yes, and I admit it now.

P. Why, then, they do what they would.

S. That I deny.

P. But they do what they think best?

S. That I admit.

P. You are talking, Socrates, in a reckless
and most extraordinary fashion.

S. Do not accuse me, most polished Polus,[25]

if I may address you after your own style. If you know how to question me, prove me in the wrong; if not, answer yourself.

P. I am very glad indeed to answer, in the hope of finding out what you mean.

[467 C – 468 C By a series of questionings, Socrates soon gets Polus to recognize three classes of things, two of which may be called positive, comprehending all things good or evil, such as health, riches, wisdom, and their opposites; while the third is neutral, including every action which, being neither good nor bad in itself, is undertaken solely for the sake of some benefit expected to accrue therefrom. Such are the acts of sitting, walking, running, and sailing; such also is medicine, the object of which is health, or traffic engaged in with the expectancy of gain. In like manner we cause a man to be put to death or sent into exile or despoiled of his possessions, only when we expect to derive some benefit through the injury we have inflicted upon him. Here Polus, beginning to see the drift of the questions which he has unsuspectingly answered, tries to avoid the inevitable conclusion, that men desire the good alone, and not the evil or even the merely neutral. Socrates, however, will not thus be turned aside, but demands a direct reply.]

S. Does what I am saying, Polus, seem to you true or not? Why do you not answer?

P. True.

S. Well, this being admitted, suppose some man, either a tyrant or a rhetorician, puts another to death, or casts him out of the city, or despoils him of his possessions, under the impression that this is for his own advantage, when it is really to his injury, he is undoubtedly doing what he sees fit, is he not?

P. Yes.

S. But is it also what he would, if it happens to be to his own injury? Why do you not answer?

P. Well, no, he does not seem to me to be doing what he would.

S. And can a man of this sort possibly have great power in the city we spoke of, if great power is a good, as by your own admission it is?

P. No, he cannot.

S. So I spoke truly when I said that it is possible for a man to do what he sees fit in a city, and at the same time neither have great power nor do what he would.

P. Just as if you yourself, Socrates, would not prefer to have liberty to do what you please in the city rather than otherwise, and are not envious of a man when you see that he has put to death or deprived of his property or sent to prison a man whom he sees fit to injure!

S. Justly, do you mean, or unjustly?

469 *P.* Whichever way he does it, is he not to be envied in either case?

S. Hush, Polus.

P. And why, pray?

S. Because we ought not to envy the unenviable or the wretched, but pity them.

P. What! do you think that it is thus with the men I speak of?

S. How can it be otherwise?

P. And so, whoever puts to death any one he sees fit, and does it justly, seems to you a wretched and pitiable object?

S. Nay, not that, but certainly not to be envied.

P. But did you not say just now that he was wretched?

S. Yes, my friend, if he has put any one to death unjustly, in which case he is pitiable as well; but he who has done it justly is not to be envied either.

P. I suppose you at least admit that the man who is unjustly put to death is wretched and pitiable.

S. Less so than he who puts him to death, Polus, and less so than he who is put to death justly.

P. How do you make that out, Socrates?

S. In this way, that to commit injustice is the greatest of evils.

P. What, this the greatest! Is not to suffer injustice a greater?

S. By no means.

P. And you would wish to suffer an injustice rather than to inflict it?

S. I should *wish* neither; but if I must needs either commit or suffer injustice, I should choose rather to suffer than to commit it.

P. And you would not be a tyrant if you could?

S. No, if by being a tyrant you mean what I do.

P. I mean by it just what I said before: being at liberty to do whatever one sees fit in the state, to put men to death and send them into exile, and to do exactly what one has a mind to do.

S. And now, esteemed sir, let me say my say, and then do you attack it. Suppose that I should appear in the midst of the crowded market-place, with a dagger concealed under my arm,[26] and thus address you: "Polus, but this moment there has come upon me a strange sort of tyrannic power. Know, if it be my good pleasure that any one of these men whom you see before you die on the instant, die he shall, no matter who he may be. And if it please me that one of them have his head broken, broken it shall straightway be; or that he have his cloak rent asunder, forthwith it shall be rent. So vast is my power in this city." And if, seeing you incredulous, I were to show you the dagger, you would very likely say when you saw it:

"Aye, Socrates, in this manner every one might have great power; for after such fashion you might burn any house you saw fit, and even the dockyards of Athens, and the galleys, and all the shipping, both public and private." But after all, Polus, this is not having great power, simply to do whatever one sees fit, do you think it is?

P. No, at least not after this fashion.

470 *S.* And can you explain what fault you have to find with this kind of power?

P. That I can.

S. Well, what is it? Tell me.

P. Because any man behaving thus would inevitably be punished.

S. And it is a bad thing to be punished, is it not?

P. Very bad.

S. And so, esteemed sir, you have come back to your former opinion, that only when doing what one sees fit is coupled with doing what is for one's advantage is it good to have great power, and that this, apparently, is what great power consists in, since power without this is but weak and harmful. But let us look at it in this way also. We are agreed, I believe, that it is sometimes better to do what we have just said, — put men to death, or banish them from our cities, or seize upon their property, — and sometimes not.

P. To be sure.

S. So far then, it seems, you and I are agreed.

P. Yes.

S. And when do you call it better to do these things? Tell me where you draw the line.

P. Here, Socrates, you had better do the answering and the questioning as well.

S. Very good, Polus, since you prefer listening to me. I call it better when these things are done justly, and worse when they are done unjustly.

P. Truly, Socrates, it is a hard matter to refute you! Why, could not even a child convict you here of not speaking the truth?

S. In that case I shall be very grateful to the child, and equally so to you, if you will refute me and set me free from my folly. Pray, then, do not weary of doing a friend a good turn, but refute me.

P. Well, indeed, Socrates, there is no need to bring up old-time events wherewith to refute you, for those that happened only the other day are quite sufficient to refute you, and to prove that many men who act unjustly are happy.

S. What events do you mean?

P. You see, I suppose, that this Archelaus, the son of Perdiccas,[27] is now ruling over Macedonia?

S. If not that, at least I hear it.

P. Well, do you look upon him as happy or miserable?

S. I do not know, Polus, for as yet I have had no intercourse with the man.

P. What! Must you needs learn it from actual intercourse with him, and do you not know, from the nature of the case, that he is happy?

S. By Zeus, I certainly do not.

P. Then it is plain, Socrates, that you will soon be saying you do not *know* that even the great king himself is happy.

S. And I shall be speaking the truth, for I do not know anything about his moral character or his training.

P. Why, does all happiness lie in this?

S. That is what I maintain, Polus. The man or woman [28] who is good and true I call happy, the base and unjust I call miserable.

P. This same Archelaus is miserable, then, in your opinion, is he?

S. If he is wicked, my friend, yes.

P. And what can he be called if not unjust? Why, the kingdom which he is now ruling did not belong to him at all, since he was born of a slave-woman of Alcetas, the brother of Perdiccas, and was by right the slave of Alcetas, so that had he desired to do that which is right he would have served Alcetas and been happy according to your notion. But as it is, he must be passing wretched, for he is guilty of the greatest crimes. The first thing he did was to summon this very master and uncle of his, under pretext of giving him back the kingdom which Perdiccas had wrested from him, and after feasting him and his son Alexander, who was cousin to himself and about his own age, and making both drunk, he threw them into a cart, and, conveying them thence by night, murdered and made way with them. And after committing these crimes, he remained unconscious of his own wretchedness and did not repent himself, nor did he choose to make himself happy by properly educating his brother, a seven-year old child and the legitimate son of Perdiccas, and restoring to him his kingdom; but shortly after he threw the boy into a well and drowned him, and then told his mother, Cleopatra, that in chasing a goose he had fallen in and perished. Wherefore, seeing he is guilty of greater crimes than any other man in Macedonia, he is the most wretched of all the Macedonians, not the happiest; and there is doubtless many a one amongst the Athenians, yourself to begin with, who would prefer to change places with any other Macedonian rather than Archelaus.

S. At the outset of our conversation, Polus, I commended you for the proficiency which I thought you showed in rhetoric, although dialectics, it seemed to me, you had neglected. And now, this is the argument, is it, with which even a child might refute me, and it is by this that you suppose I can be refuted in my assertion that the unjust man is not the happy one! And why do you think so, my friend? I assure you there is not a single thing you have said to which I agree!

P. Because you *will* not; for you really believe as I say.

S. My dear sir, you are attempting, I see, to refute me in rhetorical fashion, just as they of the law courts fancy themselves able to refute. For there, the one side think they have refuted the other, if they are able to bring forward a great number of respectable men to bear them witness in whatever statements they make, while the opposite side are able to bring forward only some single witness, or none at all. But a refutation of this kind has no value whatever in respect of the truth; for it might be that many men of good repute would bear false witness against another. And so in this matter, if you choose to bring up witnesses to testify that what I say is not true, pretty nearly every Athenian and stranger, too, will side with you. There is Nicias, the son of Niceratus,[29] who will bear you witness if you like, and his brothers with him, they whose tripods stand side by side in the place of Dionysus; or, if you like, there is Aristocrates, the son of Scellias, he who presented that beautiful offering at Delphi; or the whole house of Pericles, if you will, or indeed any other of our families that you may select. But I, though I stand alone, do not yield my assent. For you do not compel belief; you do but bring up a host of false witnesses whereby you think to drive me from my own belonging, — even the Truth. But for my own part, unless I can bring you yourself forward as my one witness to bear testimony to what I say, I deem that I shall have made no progress worth mentioning in the matter under discussion; nor to my mind will you either, unless I alone by myself bear you witness, and you let all the others go their way. There is then this one kind of refutation which you and many others believe in, and there is another in which I myself believe. Let us, therefore, place the two side by side, and see if they differ in any way one from the other. For these questions upon which we are at issue are of no slight import, but those which it is perhaps the noblest thing in the world rightly to understand, and the most disgraceful not to understand; for the upshot of the whole consists in knowing or not knowing who is the happy man and who is not. In the present case, for instance, you believe it possible for one who commits acts of injustice and is unjust to be a happy man, — that is, if you believe Archelaus to be unjust and yet happy. This is what we are to suppose you believe, is it not?

P. Certainly.

S. And I declare it to be impossible. Here, then, is one point upon which we are at issue.

Very well. And now, can a wrongdoer be happy if he suffers the penalty and is punished?

P. Far from it. In that case he would be most wretched.

S. But yet, according to your view, the wrongdoer is happy, if he suffer no penalty.

P. Yes.

S. And to my mind, Polus, the unjust man and the wrongdoer is wretched in any case; still more wretched, however, if he does not pay the penalty and suffer the punishment of his sins, less wretched if he does pay it and suffer punishment at the hands of gods and men.

P. These are sheer absurdities, Socrates, which you are trying to maintain.

S. And yet I shall try to make you maintain them with me, my good friend, for a friend I believe you to be. These, then, are the points upon which we differ. Look at them with me. Some time since I said, I believe, that to commit injustice is worse than to suffer it.

P. To be sure you did.

S. And you, that to suffer it was worse.

P. Yes.

S. And I maintained that wrongdoers are wretched, and was refuted by you.

P. Aye, by Zeus.

S. In your own opinion, Polus.

P. Which opinion I think I may say is true.

S. You, on the other hand, maintain that wrongdoers are happy, provided they pay no penalty.

P. To be sure I do.

S. And I maintain that these are most wretched; those who pay the penalty, less so. Do you wish to refute this, too?

P. Really, Socrates, this is still harder to refute than the other.

S. Not harder, Polus, but impossible; for the truth can never be refuted.

P. What do you mean? Suppose a man is detected unlawfully plotting to obtain despotic power, and, being detected, is put on the rack and hacked in pieces and has his eyes burned out, and after suffering all manner of other grievous outrages and seeing his children and his wife made to suffer the same, is finally crucified or burned to death in pitch,[30] — do you mean to say that such a man will be happier than if he were to get off free, and set himself up as tyrant, and spend the rest of his life as ruler in the city, doing whatever he pleases, envied and accounted happy by his fellow citizens and by foreigners as well? This, do you say, it is impossible to refute?

S. This time, most honourable Polus, it is bugbears[31] you are conjuring up instead of refuting me; awhile ago it was witnesses. But pray jog my memory a little. "Unlawfully plotting to obtain despotic power," you said; did you not?

P. I did.

S. Well, *happier* neither of the two can

ever be, neither he who has unlawfully acquired the power nor he who has been punished, for since the two are wretched, there can be no question of either being *happier*. Nevertheless, he who gets off free and exercises despotic power is the more wretched. How is this, Polus? Are you laughing? What new kind of refutation is this, when any one makes a statement, to laugh at him, and not attempt to refute it?

P. And do you not regard yourself as refuted, Socrates, when the statements you make are such as no man alive would grant? Just ask any one of the present company.

S. I am no statesman, Polus, and last year, when I was appointed by lot a member of the Senate, and my tribe had the presidency, and I had to put a question to vote, a laugh was raised at my expense because I did not know how to do it.[32] So do not now, I beg of you, bid me take the votes of those present; but, as I said just now, unless you have some better proof than votes, hand the matter over to me in my turn, and try the proof which I believe to be the right one. For one witness to the truth of what I say I do know how to summon, him, namely, with whom I hold the argument; the others I let alone. And one man's vote I know how to take; to all the others I have nothing to say. Consider then, whether you in your turn are willing to submit to the test and to answer my questions. For I believe that both I myself and you and all other men do regard it as a worse thing to commit injustice than to suffer it, and worse not to pay the penalty of sin than to pay it.

P. And I, that neither I nor any other man at all does so regard it. Why, would you yourself prefer to be injured rather than to injure?

S. Yes. And so would you, and so would every one.

P. Quite the contrary, neither would I myself, nor you, nor any one else.

S. Well then, will you answer my questions?

P. Indeed I will, for I am eager to know what you can possibly find to say.

[474 C – 479 A   Polus readily enough assents to the proposition that whether it be worse (more harmful) or not to commit an injury than to suffer one, it is nevertheless baser (more dishonourable); and to the question which succeeds — whether fair or honourable action does not consist of what is either useful or pleasant to him who commits it — he yields a delighted assent, not perceiving that a second admission is hereby involved, namely, that what is base is necessarily injurious or else harmful, in the same degree that what is fair is useful or pleasant; so that even were it true that to commit injustice is not painful, it is certainly injurious: and thus injustice, besides being more base, turns out to be likewise more harmful to him who commits it than to him upon whom it is committed. "And can it be," exclaims Socrates, "that you would prefer the more harmful and dishonourable thing to that which is less so? Do not shrink, Polus, from giving an answer, for it will do you no harm. Nay, rather give yourself up unflinchingly to the argument as to a surgeon, and answer me 'yes' or 'no.'" Thus exhorted, Polus, albeit with tolerably bad grace, admits the harmfulness of wrong doing. The point now to be considered is whether, the offence being once committed, it is a greater evil to suffer for it or to avoid punishment. Socrates soon extracts the admission that the character of any result depends upon the character of the action by which this result has been brought about. Just as the suffering caused by a blow is in proportion to the force with which it was dealt, so the effect of punishment corresponds to the manner of its infliction. When it is justly inflicted it is justly suffered; and when justly, then fairly; and this, inasmuch as the fair is either pleasant or useful, is necessarily a good to the sufferer.

Now, there are three great evils, — disease, which seeks relief at the hand of the physician, poverty, from which the art of money making brings release, and wrong doing, which nought but punishment can expiate ; and since of these three wrong doing is the greatest, it follows that next happiest to the man who has never harboured evil within his soul, is he who, through the ministration of justice, has found release from evil. Wherefore those who, like Archelaus, commit the greatest crimes and escape with impunity are of all men most miserable.]

S. Indeed, my good friend, such men as these might almost be said to have behaved like one who is a prey to the most grievous diseases, and yet contrives not to pay the physicians any penalty for these sins of his body, nor be healed, fearing, like a very child, to let himself be burned and cut, because, forsooth, the process is painful. Or do you not agree with me in thinking this ?

P. Certainly I do.

S. Because he does not know, apparently, what bodily health and soundness are. And it would appear, Polus, from these conclusions of ours, that they who try to flee from the penalty of their sins are doing something akin to this, for they perceive only the pain, but are blind to the usefulness, and do not know how much less wretched it is to be linked to an unsound body than to a soul that is not sound, but corrupt and unjust and unholy. Wherefore they go to all lengths that they may not suffer punishment and thus obtain release from the greatest of evils, to this end securing for themselves possessions and friends and every possible means of speaking in the most persuasive manner. But if the conclusions we have reached, Polus, be true, do you not perceive all that follows from the argument? Or shall we rather work it out together?

P. Yes, unless you prefer some other way.

S. Does it not follow, then, that injustice or wrong doing is the greatest of all evils?

P. So it appears.

S. And has it not furthermore been shown that to pay the penalty of sin is a release from this evil?

P. I suppose so.

S. And that not to pay it is to abide in the evil?

P. Yes.

S. Wrong doing, then, is only second in degree among evils; but not to pay the penalty of wrong doing is of all evils the first and greatest.

P. So it seems.

S. And is not this, my friend, the very point upon which we have been at issue, you accounting Archelaus happy, the man who, though guilty of the greatest acts of injustice, has suffered no penalty; I, on the contrary, believing that Archelaus, or any other man at all who pays not the penalty of his injustice, is more wretched far than all other men, and that he who commits the injustice is always more wretched than he who suffers it, he who does not pay the penalty than he who does pay it. Were not these the assertions I made?

P. Yes.

S. And is it not proved that I was right in making them?

P. I suppose so.

480 *S.* Very good. Now then, Polus, if all this be true, what is the great use of rhetoric? For certainly, judging from the conclusions we have reached, it behooves a man to keep the strictest possible watch over himself lest he act unjustly and thereby bring upon himself some grievous evil. Is it not so?

P. Certainly.

S. And if either he himself or any one else for whom he cares act unjustly, then must he of his own free will go where, as soon as may be, he shall meet his penalty. He must go to the judge as he would to the doctor, making all speed lest the malady of injustice be rendered chronic, and his soul become unsound to the core and past healing. What but this can we say, Polus, if our previous admissions still hold good? Is it not in this way, and no other, that these last can be brought into unison with them?

P. What else, indeed, Socrates, can we say?

S. To the end, therefore, of pleading excuse for sin, whether committed by one's self, or by one's parents or friends or children, or by one's own country, rhetoric, Polus, is of no use to us; unless, indeed, it be assumed that a man ought to accuse first himself and afterwards his kinsfolk and his friends, if at any time one of these have been guilty of injustice, attempting no concealment of the sin, but bringing it to the light, in order that by suffering the penalty he may regain health; insisting, moreover, that neither he himself nor any of the others shall play the coward, but that he shall yield himself up bravely and with blinded eyes, as to a surgeon, to be cut or cauterized, and in his pursuit of the good and noble shall take no pain into account, but give himself up to be beaten if the sin he has committed be deserving of blows, or to be sent to prison if it deserves chains, if a fine, to be fined, if exile, to be banished, if death, to die, he being foremost to accuse himself and those of his own kin, and using his oratory to the end that their deeds may be made manifest, and they be delivered from the greatest of all evils, injustice. Do we say yes to this, Polus, or do we not?

P. Strange sayings these, Socrates, it seems to me! but I suppose they tally with the statements you made before.

S. Well, must not either those statements be disproved, or else these follow of necessity?

P. Yes, that is a fact.

S. And now, looking at it again from the other side, if you have to do some one a harm — it matters not whether he be an enemy of your own or not, if only you be not the one who is injured, for that of course is to be avoided;[38] but assuming another man to have been the victim — then you should in every way, 481, both by speech and action, lay your plans to make him escape the penalty and not be brought before the judge. Or if he be brought there, then you should so contrive that the enemy, instead of suffering the penalty, shall make good his escape; and if he has gained great riches by plunder, that he keep instead of restoring them, squandering them upon himself and his friends in unjust and ungodly fashion; and if the injustice he has committed be worthy of death, that he be not suffered to die for it, — no, never, if possible, — but that he continue immortal in his wickedness, or if this may not be, that he live as long as possible, just as he is. It is to such ends as these, Polus, that oratory seems to me useful, but to one who does not intend to commit injustice there is in my opinion no great use for it; if, indeed, there be any use at all, for certainly so far none has been made apparent.

C. Tell me, Chaerephon, is Socrates in earnest about this, or in jest?

Ch. He seems to me, Callicles, to be uncommonly in earnest. However, there is nothing like asking the man himself.

C. By the gods, that is just what I am eager to do. Tell me, Socrates, are we to set you down now as in earnest, or in jest? For, if you are in earnest, and if what you say is true, would not this life of ours be turned completely upside down, and are we not apparently doing the very opposite of what we ought?

S. Were it not, Callicles, for certain experiences which, in one shape to some men, to others in another, are common to all, — were the experiences of each one of us peculiar to himself, and different from those of everybody else, — it would be no easy matter to make another understand one's own experience. I say this, remembering that you and I have had the same experience, both of us being in love, each with two objects, I with Alcibiades, the son of Cleinias, and with philosophy, you with the Demus (people) of Athens, and with Demus, the son of Pyrilampes.[34] Now, I have constantly observed that, for all your being so masterful, whatever either of your favourites may say and however he may say a matter stands, you are never able to oppose him, but are always shifting your ground backwards and forwards. In the Assembly, if you have made some assertion which the Demus of Athens disputes, you veer about and say whatever suits his pleasure, and with this fair son of Pyrilampes you do the same thing. You find it impossible to withstand the words and the counsels of your favourites, insomuch that if any one were to express surprise at the nonsense you are constantly talking just for their pleasure, you would probably inform him, if you were willing to speak the truth, that unless somebody will put a stop to 482 your favourites' saying such things, you will never stop saying them. Make up your mind, then, that this is the kind of answer you will get from me; and instead of wondering that I talk in this way, stop philosophy, my favourite, from talking thus. For she, my dear friend, is ever repeating the words you have heard from me; and she, of all my favourites, is the least fickle by far. The son of Cleinias indeed, of whom we spoke, is now of one mind, now of another, but philosophy is ever of the same mind; and these are her assertions at which you now wonder, although you yourself were present when they were made. Either then, as I have said before, refute what she said, that to commit injustice and not pay the penalty is the uttermost of evils ; or if you let this go unrefuted, I swear, Callicles, by the dog, the God of the Egyptians, that Callicles shall not agree with you, but shall be at discord with you all the days of his life. In truth, my friend, to my mind it were better for me that my lyre or any chorus of my training were out of tune and gave forth discords,[35] and better that the mass of men disagreed with me and contradicted me, — better all this, than that I, one man alone, should be at discord with myself and contradict myself.

C. Methinks, Socrates, you are running riot with the argument, like the genuine ranter you are. And you are ranting now in this fashion, because Polus has allowed himself to be treated just as he blamed Gorgias for letting you treat him. For the assertion Polus made was, I believe, that when Gorgias was asked by you whether if a man came to him who wanted to learn rhetoric but had no knowledge of justice he would impart this knowledge, he was shamed into declaring that he would, and this out of mere deference to public sentiment, which would be offended if any one were to say he would not; and that in consequence of this admission he was forced to contradict himself, and you, of course, were delighted. And at that time it was you whom Polus was turning into ridicule, — rightly, too, I think, — whereas he now in his turn has met with the same fate; and this is the very reason why I do not admire Polus, because he has given in to your assertion that it is baser to commit injustice than to suffer it. For in consequence of this admission he in his turn got entangled in the net you spread for him, and what he had to say was cut short because he was ashamed to speak his own mind. The fact is, Socrates, that, under pre-

tence of pursuing the truth, you are always leading up to vulgar and fallacious notions of this kind, fair not by nature, but only by convention. For these two, nature and convention, are for the most part opposed one to the
483 other, so that when a man is ashamed and dares not say what he thinks, he must of necessity fall into self-contradiction. And this precisely is the sly trick you have invented to twist the argument: if a man uses terms in their conventional meaning, you ask a question taking them in their natural sense; if he uses them in their natural sense, you slip in a conventional meaning. For instance, in this present matter of committing and suffering injustice, when Polus was speaking of that which is conventionally more base, you followed up his "conventionally" with your "according to nature." For if you go by nature, everything which is worse, such as suffering injustice, is likewise baser; only by convention is it baser to commit injustice. For this suffering injustice is the part not of a free man, but of a slave, for whom to die is better than to live, who, downtrodden and abused, has no power to help either himself or any one else for whom he cares. But my belief is that they who make the laws, that is, the majority, are the really weak men. It is therefore with a view to themselves and to their own interest that they make the laws and bestow praise and deal out blame; and in order

to frighten off the bolder sort of men and to prevent their gaining the advantage which they might otherwise have, they declare that it is base and unjust to claim any advantage at all, and that striving to get the advantage over others is precisely what constitutes injustice. And well, I think, may they be content, inferior as they are, to find themselves on an equality with the others.

Thus has come about the conventional saying that trying to get more than others is unjust and base, and this is what is called acting unjustly; whereas nature, it seems to me, shows us that it is right for the better man to have more than the inferior, the more powerful more than the less powerful. And in divers places, both in the animal races and amongst men, throughout whole states and tribes together, she makes it manifest that this is true, and that justice is held to consist in the superior ruling over the inferior and taking advantage of them. In virtue of what right, I should like to know, did Xerxes lead an army against Greece, or his father against the Scythians, not to mention a thousand other instances of the kind which I might name. Nay, my belief is that these deeds are enacted because they are according to nature,—aye, by Zeus, and according to the law of nature, though not the same law, I grant you, as that which we impose when we mould into shape the best and manliest amongst us, whom we take from childhood like young lions,[36] and break their spirit by means of enchantments and spells, telling them that all must have an equal share, and that this is what is fair and just. But my belief is, that if ever there appears among them a man of sufficient spirit, he will shake off all these trammels, and tear them asunder and burst away from them, and trampling under foot all these our written rules and magic arts and incantations, and such laws as are against nature, our slave shall confront us and stand forth our master, and then shall shine forth clearly that which by nature is just. Pindar, I think, brings out exactly what I mean in that ode where he says that "Law is the king of all, both mortals and immortals." "Moreover," he continues, "deeds the most violent he justifies, plundering with powerful hand; as proof whereof behold the deeds of Heracles ; for all unbought —." It runs something like that, although I do not know the ode by heart. At all events, he goes on to say that, although the oxen had been neither given nor sold to him by Geryon, he carried them off, assuming that this was his natural right, and that oxen and all other possessions belonging to the weaker and inferior are the property of the stronger and superior.[87]

That this is the truth of the case you shall learn, if you will let philosophy alone and pass on to higher matters. For philosophy, Socrates, is a pleasing thing enough if a man engages in it moderately and at the proper age; but if he lingers over it longer than he ought, it becomes his ruin. For however great may be his natural parts, if he goes on with philosophy beyond the proper age, he must of necessity find himself without experience in all the matters in which that man must be versed who would be a citizen of worth and eminence.[38] For men such as these know nothing of the laws of the state or of the terms used in all kinds of dealings with other men, whether private or public, or of the pleasures and desires of men; in short, they are altogether unacquainted with the humanities of life. Whenever, then, they enter upon any transaction, whether private or public, they make themselves ridiculous; just as public men, I dare say, become ridiculous whenever they in their turn enter into your pursuits and discussions. For it is as Euripides says:—

"Each man in that doth shine, and that pursue,
And the best hours of day to that devote
Wherein he may the most excel himself."

485 But in whatever thing he finds himself deficient, that he avoids and decries, while the thing wherein he excels he praises out of pure self-love, thinking thus to gain praise for himself. But to my thinking the best way is to have some share in both of these. To have enough philosophy to complete one's general training is an excellent thing, and it is no dis-

grace for a lad to dabble in it. But when it comes to a man already advanced in years who still keeps on with philosophy, the thing, Socrates, becomes ridiculous, and I, for my part, feel towards those who continue to pursue it very much as I do towards those who lisp and behave in other respects like children. For when I see a child, whom this way of speaking yet befits, lisping as he plays about, I am charmed, and think it pleasing and unaffected and suited to his childish years; nay, when I hear some little creature speak distinctly, it is disagreeable to me and wounds my ears, and I find in it something slavishly mechanical. But when we hear a man lisp or see him behaving himself like a child, we feel that he is putting himself in a ridiculous and unmanly light and deserves a good beating. Now this is just what I feel in regard to those who follow philosophy. When I see a young lad with a taste for philosophy, I am well pleased and regard it as becoming, and such a one I set down as a true freeman; while he who takes no interest in philosophy seems to me a slavish creature, who will never deem himself capable of any high or noble action. But when I see an old fellow who still goes on with philosophy, instead of leaving it behind him, that man, Socrates, seems to me to deserve a beating on the spot. For, as I said just now, one of that sort, however well endowed by nature, if he avoids the heart of the city and the public places where, as the poet says, men acquire eminence,[39] must necessarily become unmanly; and accordingly he skulks away and passes the rest of his life in a corner, whispering into the ear of three or four youths, but never raising his voice to utter a word that is great or sound or worthy of a freeman.

Now, I, Socrates, am really very well disposed towards you; indeed, I feel very much as Zethus did towards Amphion in that passage of Euripides of which I reminded you. And I am impelled to address to you the very same reproaches which he addressed to his brother, that you, Socrates, pay no heed to the things for which you ought to care,[40] but clothe a soul noble by nature in a kind of puerile disguise, and in a court of justice could neither state a case aright, nor devise aught plausible and persuasive, nor make any stout-hearted resolve in behalf of another. Wherefore tell me truly, my dear Socrates, and do not get angry with me, for I speak out of kindness to you, does it not seem to you a disgraceful thing to be in such case as I believe not you alone but all others to be in who are forever delving into the depths of philosophy? Only suppose that some one were to seize you or any one else of your own sort, and drag you off to prison, declaring you guilty of a crime which you had not committed at all: you know well enough that you could do nothing to help yourself, but would stand there with swimming head and open mouth, and never a word to say; and when you came to appear before the court, however mean and low your accuser, you would have to die, if he chose that death should be your penalty. And how, Socrates, can that art be wise which converts a man of fine parts into an inferior creature, incapable of helping himself or of saving either his own life or that of any one else from the greatest dangers, and leaves him to be stripped by his enemies of all his substance and to live as a complete outlaw in the state? Such a one as this, if it be not unmannerly so to speak, any man may slap in the face and not be called to account for it.[41] Nay, my friend, yield to my counsels; leave off this habit of refuting, and practice the art of dealing with realities, and practice also that which shall gain you a reputation for common sense, leaving to other men these over-niceties, whether they are to be called follies or nonsense, whereby you will only be brought to dwell in an empty house;[42] and emulate not the men who spend their time in probing these insignificant questions, but rather those who possess means and reputation and all the other good things of life.

S. Had it so chanced, Callicles, that my soul were made of gold, should I not, think you, have rejoiced to discover one of those stones, the best one of its kind, whereby gold is tested, that I might apply my soul to it, and, if it assured me that my soul had been trained aright, might then know myself to be in sound condition, and in need of no further test?

C. What is your object, Socrates, in asking this?

S. I will tell you presently. In you I believe that I have found such a touchstone.

C. How so?

S. Because I know very well that if you assent to any one of my soul's beliefs they must be surely true. For I am convinced that he who desires thoroughly to test a soul and know whether or not it lives aright, must possess three qualities, all of which you do possess — knowledge and good-will and assurance. Many people I meet who are not capable of testing me, because they are not clever like you; while others there are who, though clever enough, are not willing to tell me the truth, because they do not care for me as you do. These very two guests of ours, Gorgias and Polus, are clever enough, to be sure, and are also kindly disposed towards me, but they are deficient in assurance, and far more diffident than they should be. How, indeed, can this be denied, when so far have they carried their diffidence that just on account of it each of them dares contradict his own words before a host of witnesses, and this on matters of the greatest importance? Now you possess all these qualities which the others lack, being sufficiently educated, as many of the Athenians would testify, and well disposed towards me besides. What proof have I of this? I will tell you. I am aware, Callicles, that four of you are banded together in the quest of wisdom: yourself, namely, and Tisander of Aphidnæ, and Andron the son of Androtion, and Nausicydes of Cholarges.[43] And once I heard you taking counsel together as to how far wisdom ought to be pursued, and I know that at that time some such opinion as this obtained among you, that it was not well to follow philosophy into detail; you even exhorted one another to take care lest by becoming over-wise you should unwittingly work your own ruin. When, therefore, I hear you giving me the same advice that you gave your own most intimate friends, — this to me is sufficient proof that you do truly wish me well. And that you are, moreover, capable of speaking out boldly and without diffidence you yourself declare, and this is borne out also by the speech you made just now. It is evident, therefore, that the state of the case is thus: if you assent to any of my opinions, that opinion will have been sufficiently tested by myself as well as by you, and there will be no need of applying to it any other touchstone. For you would never have agreed with me either through lack of wisdom or by reason of diffidence; nor would you have done so to deceive me, since you are my friend, as you yourself declare. Whatever, then, you and I together agree upon, that of a surety will be the perfection of truth. And of all searches, Callicles, that one is noblest which is concerned with those questions about which you took me to task, namely, what a man should 488 be, and what he should pursue, and up to what point, both in old age and in youth. For if in the conduct of my own life I do what is not right, you know very well that I err not wittingly, but because of my ignorance. Do not, then, forbear to admonish me as you began by doing, but make it clear to me what I ought to pursue, and in what way I may acquire the same; and if you detect me now holding some principle in common with you, and at some later day acting at variance with the same, you may set me down for a dolt and a good for nothing, and never admonish me again. Pray, then, go back to the beginning, and tell me how you and Pindar define natural justice. Does it mean that the stronger are to carry off by force the possessions of the weaker, and the better to rule over the worse, and the superior to have more than the inferior? Do you define justice as other than this, or does my memory serve me right?

C. Yes, that was what I said then, and what I say now.

[488 B – 489 B   Socrates now demands a closer definition of the terms "superior" and "stronger." Is the one necessarily included in the other, or is, on the contrary, superiority compatible with physical weakness, inferiority with bodily strength? With great decision Callicles pronounces superiority and strength to be identical. But, answers Socrates, since, "according to the law of nature," the physically stronger are also the superior, they who are in the majority must needs be right. Now, in the opinion of the majority, to commit injustice is more ignoble than to suffer it; hence it follows that the self-same thing which Callicles has previously declared to be a mere convention is now out of his very mouth proved to be the truth, and this according to "nature," not "convention."

Here, Callicles attempts to escape the consequences of his ill-fated assertion by changing the definition of his terms.]

C. This fellow never will have done trifling! Tell me, Socrates, are you not ashamed, at your age, to be always on the hunt after words, — if a man happens to make a slip in an expression, looking upon it as a godsend? Do you suppose that by the superior I mean any but the better? Have I not been telling you this long time that to me the superior and the better are the same? You do not suppose I mean, do you, that if any rabble of slaves and all manner of men who are of no account whatever, save perhaps in the way of physical strength, get together and make any statement they please, the same is law?

S. Very good, most wise Callicles. So this is the view you take, is it?

C. Of course it is.

S. Well, my dear sir, I myself have been for some time conjecturing that by the superior you did mean something of this kind; but I am putting the question again, because I am eager to know exactly what your meaning is. For I do not really suppose you believe that two men must be better than one, or that your slaves are better than you because forsooth they are stronger. But I wish you would go back to the beginning and say what you do mean by the better, since it is not the stronger. And do, pray, my good sir, instruct me a little more mildly, if you would not have me run away from your school.

C. You are pleased to be sarcastic, Socrates.

S. Not so, Callicles, by that Zethus under cover of whom you were just now launching so many sarcasms against me. But come, tell us whom you do call the better?

C. The better sort of men, of course.

S. There, do you not see that after all you yourself are only repeating words and not explaining anything! Will you not say whether by the better and the superior you mean any other than those who have more practical wisdom?

C. I mean those, by Zeus; most distinctly I do.

490 *S.* Frequently then, judging by what you say, one wise man will be superior to ten thousand who are not wise, and he it is who should rule, while the others should be ruled; and he who rules should have the advantage of those who are ruled. This, as I understand it, is what you would say — and, believe me, I am not word-hunting — if the one be superior to the ten thousand.

C. Yes, that is what I mean. For I believe that natural justice consists in letting the better and wiser man rule over his inferiors and have the advantage over them.

S. Wait a minute. What is this you are saying now? Just suppose that we are, as at this moment, a goodly number of men together, and that we have in common a quantity of food and drink, and that we are of every sort and kind, some strong, others weak; but that one of us, being a physician, has more knowledge of these particular matters, although in other respects he is probably like the rest of us, — stronger than some, weaker than others, — would not he, having more knowledge than ourselves, be our better and superior as to these matters?

C. Certainly.

S. Ought he, then, to have a larger share of this food than the rest of us, because he is better; or ought he, in virtue of his authority, to have absolute control of its distribution, but, in the matter of consuming and using it for his own body, to take, if he would be free from blame, no more than falls to his share, which would be larger than the portion of some, smaller than that of others; in such wise that if he happens to be the weakest of the whole, the smallest share of all will fall to the best man, Callicles? Is it not so, my good fellow?

C. You talk of food, and drink, and physicians, and all such stuff; but I am not talking about these.

S. Well, do you mean that the wiser is the better man? Answer me, "yes" or "no."

C. Yes, I do.

S. But surely, you think that the better man should have the larger share?

C. Not of food, nor of drink either.

S. Oh, I see; you mean of clothes, I suppose. And so the best weaver is to have the largest cloak, and go about clad in the finest cloaks and the largest number of the same.

C. Who talks of cloaks?

S. But in the matter of shoes, at least, it is plain that the best and most intelligent maker of these is to have the largest share. The shoemaker, of course, is to go about shod in the biggest shoes, and the largest number of them.

C. Who talks of shoes? You will persist in your nonsense.

S. Well, if you do not mean that sort of thing, it is probably something of this kind. A husbandman, for instance, who has a practical and thorough knowledge of land, is to have, I suppose, a larger share of the seeds, and to use the largest quantity of them upon his own land.

C. How you do keep saying over the same thing, Socrates!

S. Not only the same thing, Callicles, but upon the same subjects also.

C. Yes, by the gods, you literally never have done harping on the subject of cobblers, and fullers, and cooks, and doctors, just as if our discussion had anything to do with these.[44]

S. But why do you not tell us what the things are of which the better and wiser man is entitled to have a larger share? or do you intend neither to accept my suggestions, nor to make any yourself?

C. Why, I have been telling you this long time. In the first place, by the superior I mean not cobblers, nor cooks either, but such as have a knowledge of state affairs and of the way in which they should be administered, and not simply knowledge, but courage as well, and hence the ability to carry through whatever they may have set their mind upon, and who will not be turned from their purpose by faintness of heart.

S. Do you observe, my dear Callicles, how different is your charge against me from mine against you? You complain that I am forever saying the same things, and take me to task for this; I, on the other hand, complain that you never say the same thing upon the same subjects, but at one time define the better and superior as the stronger, at another as the wiser; and now here again you are presenting still another view, for you declare the better and superior to be the more courageous. Now do, my friend, tell me once and for all whom you really mean by the better and superior, and in what they are so.

C. But I have already told you that I mean those who have knowledge and courage in affairs of state. These are the men to whom it belongs to rule our cities, and justice consists in their having the advantage over the others, — the rulers over those who are ruled.

S. What, over themselves, my friend! [45]

C. What do you mean?

S. I mean that every man is ruler over himself; or is it not his duty to rule himself, but only others?

C. What do you mean by ruling himself?

S. Nothing out of the common, but just what is generally meant, — being temperate, and exercising self-control, and ruling over the pleasures and the desires within himself.

C. What an innocent you are! Actually,

you are describing those simpletons, the temperate.

S. Of course I am. Any one might know that it is they I mean.

C. And simpletons they are, Socrates, with a vengeance![46] How, I ask you, can a man possibly be happy if he is in subjection to anything whatsoever? No; that which is by nature just and right is that which I now boldly proclaim it to be, — he who would live aright must allow his desires full growth, and on no account restrain them, but must, by dint of audacity and astuteness, qualify himself to minister to them when they shall have attained their fullest growth, and to gratify each appetite as it arises. But this, I suppose, is not possible to the generality of men, and so, ashamed of their own incompetency, they seek to hide it by casting reproach upon men of the other sort, and they give out that unrestraint is shameful, in order, as I said before, to bring under subjection those who are by nature the better men; and because they are unable to procure satisfaction for their own desires, they extol temperance and justice, all by reason of their own unmanliness. Those, for example, who were born the sons of kings, or those who are by nature gifted with ability to gain some kind of sovereignty or tyranny or some part in an oligarchy, — what greater evil or disgrace than temperance could there be to men of this sort?

Free as they are to enjoy good things, and with no one to hinder them, would you have them bring upon themselves the laws and opinions and censure of the mass of mankind as masters? How, indeed, can they fail of being made wretched through this noble virtue of justice and temperance, if they may award to friends no more than to enemies, and this when actually bearing rule in their own city? Nay, Socrates, by that truth which you profess to seek, the real state of the case is this: luxury and excess and license, provided they have power behind them, are virtue and happiness, and the other things you talk about, the fine speeches, the unnatural conventionalities, are all of a piece, — mere popular talk, and of no account whatever.

S. Certainly, Callicles, there is nothing half-hearted in your bold treatment of the question. You come out openly with what other men think, but are not willing to say. I beg, therefore, that you will on no account leave off until it has become clear to us how we ought to live. And tell me this; you maintain that if a man is to be what he ought, he must not restrain his desires, but allow them to attain their fullest growth, and in one way or another provide for their gratification; and this you maintain to be virtue?

C. Yes, that is what I maintain.

S. Then, they who have no wants at all cannot rightly be said to be happy?

C. No, indeed; for in that case stones and dead men were happiest of all.

S. Truly, from what you tell us, life is an awful thing. Indeed I should not be at all surprised if Euripides were right when he says :
" Who knows whether to live be not to die ?
To die to live ? " [47]

493 And perhaps in reality we are dead, just as I myself once heard from one of the wise men, that we are dead even now, and that the body is our tomb, and that the part of the soul which contains our desires is of a nature easy to be persuaded and made to drift back and forth. And a certain ingenious man, a Sicilian, I think, or an Italian, expressed this in a fable. From the credulous nature of the soul and its readiness to be persuaded, he called it, by a play on words, a vessel,[48] and the thoughtless he called uninitiated or leaky ; and the part of their souls which contains the desires, that part which is unrestrained and unretentive, he likened, on account of its insatiableness, to a vessel perforated with holes. Just the reverse, Callicles, you see, from yourself, he sets forth how in Hades — meaning, of course, the invisible world — the uninitiated must be of all most wretched, forever dipping water into their leaky vessels with a sieve equally leaky. And by the sieve, as he who told me the tale explained, he meant the soul ; and the soul of the thoughtless he likened to a sieve, because it is

as it were full of holes, and is incapable of retaining anything by reason of its unbelief and forgetfulness. Now, that there is something rather absurd about all this, I grant you; but still, it brings out the point which I wish to make clear, in order to persuade you, if I possibly can, to change your mind and, in place of the life which is insatiable and given over to excess, to choose that which is moderate and content with what it has, and satisfied with the mere necessities of life. But, tell me, is this at all convincing to you, and are you coming round to the notion that the temperate are happier than those who are given over to excess; or would any number of the like tales, were I to tell you them, have no effect in changing your mind?

C. There, Socrates, you are nearer the truth.

S. Come then, let me give you another simile belonging to the same school. See whether you would say in regard to these two lives, that of the temperate and that of the licentious man, that it is as if two men had each a certain number of jars, those belonging to the first man being sound, and filled, one with wine, one with honey, one with milk, and so on, one with one thing and one with another, although the sources of supply are so scanty and hard of access that only by long and severe labour can he keep himself supplied. This man, then, when he has once filled his jars needs not to bring further supplies or give himself any further trouble, but, so far as that goes, may take his ease ; but the other, although, like the first one, he is able to supply himself from the sources, has jars which are all unsound and full of holes, so that he must needs forever, day and night, keep on filling them, if he would not suffer the uttermost pangs. Such, then, being the life of each, do you call that of the licentious man happier than that of the moderate one ? Does this tale of mine persuade you into agreeing with me that the life of self-restraint is better than that of excess, or do I not convince you ?

C. You do not convince me, Socrates, for the man who is satisfied has no longer any pleasure left him ; in fact, it is as I said just now : to be satisfied is to live like a stone, feeling neither pleasure nor pain. No, indeed, all the pleasure of life consists in this, — in having the inflow as great as possible.

S. But if the inflow be great, must not of necessity the outflow be great also, and the holes, moreover, large enough to admit of this outflow ?

C. Of course.

S. Then you in your turn are describing the life not of a dead man or a stone, but that of a kind of cormorant.[49] Tell me, pray, do you mean such things as hunger and eating to gratify hunger ?

C. I do.

S. And thirst and drinking to gratify thirst?

C. I mean these, and having every other kind of desire as well, and being able to gratify them all, and so live a life of happiness.

S. Well said, my fine fellow. Only keep on as you have begun, and take care that you are not shamed into drawing back.

[494 C – 505 B Prefacing the coming illustration by the announcement that it requires all the boldness which he has just enjoined upon Callicles, Socrates now asks whether if a man suffering from irritability of the skin be allowed to rub himself all day long, he can be said to lead a pleasant and happy life.

Although Callicles answers in the affirmative, — being put on his mettle by a further allusion to the diffidence of Polus and Gorgias, — he shows signs of wavering as to the complete identity of pleasure and good, and when finally asked to restate his opinion upon this subject, it is with evident reluctance that he replies, "Well, lest I contradict myself if I say they are different, I declare them to be the same."

"But, Callicles," Socrates remonstrates, "you are doing away with your former assertion, and will be no longer qualified to join me in the search for truth, if you say what is contrary to your real opinion."

"Why, so do you, Socrates," is the rejoinder. Whereupon Socrates remarks: "Then I am not doing what is right, any more than you are."

Callicles no longer hesitates to reiterate his belief that good is identical with pleasure. His subsequent assertion that knowledge and courage are different from pleasure and also from one another is thus greeted by Socrates:—

"Well, let us not forget this, that Callicles the Archarnian [50] has pronounced pleasure and good to be identical, but knowledge and courage to be different from each other and also from the good."

"But Socrates of Alopece of course does not agree with us in this, or does he, perhaps?"

"He does not," is the answer, "nor will Callicles either, I think, when he shall have beheld himself truly."

The question is now raised whether opposites of any kind can exist simultaneously. Is not a man said to be in good health only when he is free from disease, or to be diseased only when not in a state of health? And is it not equally true of good and evil, happiness and wretchedness, and indeed of all other antitheses, that each in turn follows or else is followed by its opposite? "If, then," continues Socrates, "we discover opposites which simultaneously exist or cease to exist, it is evident that these cannot possibly be the good and the evil." Assured by Callicles of his "unlimited assent" to this statement, Socrates next ascertains that pleasure and pain on the contrary do exist simultaneously. When suffering, for instance, from hunger and thirst, we feel the pain of the want at the very moment of gratifying it, insomuch that no sooner does the pain cease than the pleasure of its gratification ceases also. Here Callicles impatiently exclaims: "I do not understand, Socrates, what all this hair-splitting is about!"

"Yes, you do, Callicles," is the reply, "but you choose to affect ignorance. Pray go on to the next step, that you may discover how clever you are, who are taking me to task. Do we not all of us, when we drink, get rid of thirst and of pleasure at the same moment?"

"I do not know," reiterates Callicles, "what you are talking about."

But here Gorgias comes to the rescue of the argument. "Do not, Callicles," he expostulates, "behave in this way, but answer for our sakes, that the discussion may be carried on to the end."

"But it is always the same story, Gorgias, with Socrates. He will keep on asking little, good-for-nothing questions,[61] and this is what he calls refuting."

"Well, why do you mind that? It will do you no harm, Callicles. Do, pray, let Socrates argue in whatever way he prefers."

"Go on, then, you," thus Callicles addresses

Socrates, "with your petty little questions, since Gorgias will have it so."

" You are a lucky man, Callicles," is the rejoinder, "to have been initiated into the greater mysteries before the lesser.[52] I did not know before that this was lawful."

Returning now to the charge, Socrates obtains from Callicles the confession that although the man of sense and courage, not the fool and the coward, is rightly called the good man, the coward is, nevertheless, capable of experiencing a keener pleasure or pain, at the enemy's retreat or advance in battle, than the brave man can possibly experience. And now, pleading in excuse the old adage, that "twice, nay even thrice, is it well to say over words of wisdom and pass them in review,"[53] Socrates draws the inevitable conclusion that, assuming pleasure and good to be identical, he who feels the keenest pleasure must needs be the better man, and that the coward or bad man is therefore proved to be as good or even better than the good one.

Callicles is now fairly driven off his ground, but instead of acknowledging his defeat, he contemptuously remarks : " All this time, Socrates, that I have been listening to you, and giving my assent, I have observed that the most trifling concession, even when made in jest, you cling to with delight, just as a young boy might do. As if you could really suppose that I or any other human being does not hold that some pleasures are better, others worse!" [54]

"Dear me, Callicles," Socrates exclaims, "what a sly fellow you are! Why, you treat me just as if I were a child, one moment telling me that things are so, the next that they are otherwise, as if on purpose to deceive me. How little I thought in the beginning that you, whom I took for a friend, would ever of your own free will deceive me! But I see now that I was mistaken, and apparently I must, as the saying goes, e'en make the best of what I can get, and take whatever you are pleased to grant me."

The questioning is now resumed, and soon the same conclusion follows which, with the help of Polus, was previously reached, that all our actions have good, not pleasure, for their end, and that we make choice of the latter only when we believe it likely to promote our good. To determine, however, which pleasures conduce to good and which to evil, we need, as before stated, not the empirical knowledge of the mere experimenter, but the true and well-grounded knowledge of the expert. "And, by the God of friendship," Socrates earnestly enjoins, "do not, Callicles, think yourself justified in trifling with me, or in giving hap-hazard answers contrary to your real belief, or in treating my words as a jest. For, as you can well see, this discussion of ours is upon a subject which any man with the least sense must care for beyond all others ; namely, the life we ought to live, whether that to which you exhort me, the life busied with those aforesaid 'manly affairs,' — speaking in the Assembly and practising oratory and engaging in public duties, as you conceive of them, — or the life spent in the pursuit of the philosophy, and wherein the one differs from the other."

Callicles is now reminded that medicine has already been described as able, from its knowledge of a patient's constitution, to give a reason for all it does, fancy cookery on the contrary as ignorant of the nature of the very pleasure which it seeks to provide, and only able to guess at probabilities. And he is asked whether, in the same way, there are not pursuits which aim solely at the gratification of the soul, and which, therefore, deserve to be classed, together with those which cater to the body, under the one head of "flattery." "Do you, Callicles," is the conclusion, "agree with us in this opinion, or do you oppose it?"

"Not I, forsooth ; I yield the point, that your argument may come to an end and also to oblige my friend Gorgias."

Socrates now enumerates certain pursuits which may be ranked as arts of flattery, amongst which are included dithyrambic poetry, fluteplaying, and all kinds of musical contests.[55]

"Do you suppose," he asks, "that Cinesias, the son of Meles, ponders how he can make his hearers better men, or does he think only how he may tickle the ears of the crowd? ... Or was it, think you, with a view to the improvement of his audience that Meles, his father, used to perform upon the cithara? Nor was it for their pleasure even, for his music was a torture to all who heard it. . . . Turn we now to Tragedy, the solemn and august. Does she care for the gratification of her hearers alone, or does she oppose it and never give utterance to anything, however pleasing, which may do them harm, but sing only of that which it shall profit them to hear, whether or not they find pleasure therein?"

From poetry to rhetoric or oratory the transition is not difficult. Alike, in that both are addressed to mixed audiences of men, women, and children, with a view solely to the pleasure of the hour, the latter may be regarded as poetry only divested of melody and rhythm.[56] But here Callicles demurs, urging that although of some orators this may be true, others there are who truly care for the good of their fellow-citizens. Challenged to bring forward an instance amongst those of the present day he finds himself at a loss, but when bidden to seek his example from the past he triumphantly exclaims : —

"What! Have you never heard how virtuous a man was Themistocles? and Cimon, and Miltiades, and our own Pericles, too, who died but lately?[57] Why, you yourself have listened to him."

"Yes," is the reply, "if to fulfil one's own desires and those of others be virtue, as you said at first; but if, as we have been forced to admit, there is an art which rightly discerns between those desires by the gratification of which men become better and those through which they become worse, which of these men can be said to have possessed it?" As Callicles confesses his inability to produce an instance, Socrates proposes that they search together for an example. The good orator, like the good workman, is one who sets before himself a certain standard, a regular and perfect whole, to be attained. But to this end it is necessary that a certain order be preserved, and that each part be brought into harmony with every other part. "Now what," he continues, "is that which is brought about in the body by the principles of regularity and order?"

"Health and strength I suppose you mean?"

"I do. And, now, again, what do these same principles bring about in the soul?[58] Try to find out this and declare it as you did the other."

"Why don't you declare it yourself, Socrates?"

"Oh, if you prefer it I will, of course. And

if what I say seems right, do you assent to it; if not, do not let it pass, but refute it."

These principles, Socrates now declares, beget in the soul law and lawfulness, which qualities, being none other than those of justice and temperance, it is the duty of the good and skilful statesman to implant in the souls of men, while he seeks to free them from self-indulgence and intemperance. "For is it not true," he asks, "that when the body is diseased, the physician enjoins abstinence from things which a well man may enjoy with impunity?"]

S. And is it not the same thing, good sir, with the soul? So long as she is yet in wickedness, being without intelligence or discipline or justice or holiness, she must be kept back perforce from her desires and suffered to do only such things as will make her better. Do you agree or not?

C. I do.

S. For this, I presume, is best for the soul herself?

C. By all means.

S. And is not keeping her back from the things she desires disciplining her?

C. Yes.

S. To be disciplined, then, is better for the soul than to be without discipline?

C. I do not know what you are talking about,

Socrates. You had better ask some other person.

S. Here is a man who cannot stand being benefited, and himself subjected to the very thing in question, — discipline.

C. I care not a whit for any of the things you are talking about, and it is only to please Gorgias that I have answered you.

S. Very good, but what are we to do now? Break off in the midst of the discussion?

C. You know best.

S. Well, they do say, you know, that it is not lawful to break off even stories in the midst, but that each should have a head upon it and not wander about headless.[59] Pray then go on answering, that our argument may get a head.

C. Oh, you are masterful enough, Socrates; but if you take my advice you will let this discussion alone, or pursue it with some one else.

S. Who else then is willing? For we must not think of leaving the discussion unfinished.

C. And can you not carry it through yourself, — either talking straight on, or else answering your own questions?

S. Yes; that it may be with me as Epicharmus said: "What erst two men affirmed, I must suffice for."[60] Well, I suppose it must needs be so. If, however, we do take this course, I think, for my part, that we ought all to vie one with the other to find out what is true and what is false in the questions before us, since it is

for the interest of all that this be made clear.
I will therefore go on with the argument in the way that seems to me best; and if any one of you thinks that I am making concessions to myself which are not true, let him take the opposite side and refute me. For what I say, I say not as if I were sure of it, nay, I am a fellow-searcher with you all, insomuch that if there seems to be anything in what my opponent says, I shall be the first to yield the point. This I say, in case you think it best to have the argument carried on to its close; but if you do not care for this, we will let it go and take our way home.

G. No, Socrates; it seems to me that we ought on no account to go away, but that you ought to stay and bring the argument to an end; and all the others, I think, are of the same mind. At all events, I myself am anxious to hear you go through the rest of it by yourself.

S. I assure you, Gorgias, that I would gladly have gone on talking with our friend Callicles until I had paid him back the speech of Amphion in return for his of Zethus; but since you, Callicles, are not willing to join me in bringing the discussion to an end, I beg that you will at least, as you listen, take me up if I say anything which you do not think right. And if you refute me I shall not get vexed with you as you do with me, but shall set you down as my greatest benefactor.

C. Speak on, my good fellow, by yourself, and get through with it.

[506 C – 507 A The "dialogue with himself" Socrates opens with the recapitulation of sundry conclusions which have been already reached.

Pleasure and good differ one from the other in this respect, — that good may not be pursued for the sake of pleasure, but pleasure for the sake of good.

The goodness of every created thing is due to the indwelling of some virtue peculiar to itself, which virtue is the result not of chance, but of some order inherent to itself.

The soul, therefore, which is governed by its own inherent order is better than the soul which follows no order. Now it is the soul governed by order which is temperate.[61]]

507 And the temperate soul is good, is it not? I myself, dear Callicles, can find nothing to bring up against this, but if you can, pray teach it to me.

C. Say on, my good fellow.

S. I say, then, that if the temperate soul is good, then that which is the opposite of temperate — the intemperate and undisciplined soul — is bad. . . . Of course it is. . . . And surely the temperate man would fulfil his duties towards gods and men, for he would not be temperate if he let his duties go unfulfilled. . . . This must be so. . . . And in his dealings towards men he will do what is just, in those towards the gods what is holy; and he who does what is just and holy must of necessity himself be just and holy. . . . Even so. . . . And he must, moreover, be courageous, for it is the part of the temperate man not to follow after or fly before what he ought not, but what he ought, whether occupations or people or pleasures or pains, and patiently to endure wherever there is need. Necessarily, Callicles, therefore, the temperate man, being as we have described him, just and courageous and holy, is a perfectly good man; and the good man does well and honourably all that he does; and he who does well [62] is blessed and happy, while the wicked man and he who does evil is wretched; and this were none other than the opposite of the temperate,—the man given to excess, whom you were praising.

Such, then, is my position, and I maintain it to be the true one. And if it be true, then it would appear that he who wishes to be happy should follow after temperance and practise it, and that every man of us should flee from excess, as fast as his feet will carry him; and that, above all things, he should so order himself as not to require punishment; but yet if he himself or any one of his, whether private person or city, stand in need of it, then justice and punishment must be dealt him, if he is ever to be happy. This, it seems to me, is the mark which a man ought to keep before him in his life, and to this end direct all his own efforts and those of the State, to the end that he who hopes to be happy shall keep justice and temperance ever before him, and not let his desires go unrestrained, and, in the endeavor to fulfil them — a never-ending torment[63] — lead the life of a robber. For such an one would be kindly affectioned neither towards any other man, nor towards God, for to him fellowship would be impossible; and to whom there is no fellowship, there can be no friendship either. The wise men, Callicles, tell us that heaven and 508 earth, and gods and men are knit together in fellowship and friendship and order and temperance and justice; whence it comes, my friend, that this whole universe bears the name of Cosmos (order), not that of disorder or license. But you, it seems to me, have paid no attention to these things, and, for all your being so clever, it has escaped your notice that geometrical equality can do great things among gods and men alike; for you care nothing about geometry, but believe, on the contrary, that a love of gain or inequality ought to be encouraged.[64] Very well; either this theory of ours must be refuted, that by the possession of justice and temperance the happy are made happy and by the possession of evil the wretched are made miserable, or, if it be true, we must see what are its results. The very same, Callicles, concerning which you asked me whether I was in earnest in saying that a man ought to accuse himself and his son and his friend, if any of them commit an injury, and that rhetoric must be used to this end. And so, what you imagined Polus to have conceded out of false shame turns out to have been true after all, that to inflict an injury is as much more disastrous as it is more disgraceful than to suffer one, and that he who wishes to be a true rhetorician must be just and understand about justice, which again is what Polus accuses Gorgias of having conceded out of false shame.

This being the state of the case, let us see what this reproach of yours amounts to, and whether or not you are right in saying that I am unable to help either myself or any of my friends or kinsfolk or to save them from the greatest dangers, and that, like the outlaws with whom any one may do as he chooses, I am at the mercy of everybody's will; whether that be, to use your own energetic expression, to slap me in the face or take away my possessions or drive me out of the city or even inflict the last of penalties, death, which is, according to you, the greatest disgrace of all. But, as for myself, Callicles, — and although this has been said many times already, it will still bear repeating,

— I maintain that to be slapped in the face without just cause is not the greatest disgrace, — no, nor to have my body cut nor my purse-strings either,— but that to strike or wound me or mine without just cause is worse and more disgraceful besides ; and that to steal from me, withal, and to enslave me and break into my house, in short, to commit any kind of unjust action upon me or mine, is a worse thing and a more disgraceful to him who commits the injury than to me who suffers it. These truths, which were brought out in the first part of our conversation just as I now declare them, are
509 clinched and riveted, if I may be pardoned such an extravagant expression, by arguments of iron and adamant, — at least, so they would appear,—and unless you or some one still more energetic than yourself shall succeed in breaking them, nothing contrary to what I now say can be said with truth. I, for my part, have always said the same thing, — that I do not, indeed, know the truth as to these matters, but that of all those I have ever met on previous occasions, as at present, there is none who can say anything different from this without making himself ridiculous.

[509 B - 511 A   Now, so the argument goes on, if there be really these two evils, that of suffering injustice and that of committing it, and if there be any help at hand whereby they may be avoided, that man is indeed foolish who does not avail himself of it.

In respect to suffering injustice, Callicles readily agrees that whatever "help" there is must consist in more than the *wish*, namely, in the *power* to avoid it. But to the proposition that the same is true of committing injustice he will apparently neither give nor withhold his assent until urged by Socrates as follows:—

"Will you not even tell me, Callicles, whether you think Polus and I were right in letting ourselves be forced into the acknowledgment that no one wishes to commit injustice, but that all who do so, do it against their will?"

"Be it so, Socrates, if you wish," is the reply, "anything to get through the discussion."

The most effectual "help" against injustice is soon discovered to be either to obtain absolute power for one's self, or to become the friend and associate of one possessed of this power. Well pleased, Callicles exclaims:—

"Don't you see, Socrates, how ready I am to give you praise whenever you say anything good? This I regard as uncommonly well said."

"Then see," Socrates remarks, "whether you approve of this also.

"On the principle of 'like to like' laid down by wise men of yore, the brutal and ignorant ruler selects as his friend not one superior to himself, whom he must needs hold in awe, nor again one greatly his inferior, whom he despises, but rather one who, possessing the same tastes with himself, will the more readily submit to his guidance. Hence, any youth who is seeking how he may best acquire power and escape injury should cultivate the same tastes with the tyrant, his lord and master, and imitate him by committing every possible injustice and avoiding punishment, which imitation will surely result in the greatest evil that could befall him — the depravity and corruption of his soul."

Here Callicles indignantly exclaims : —]

C. I cannot conceive, Socrates, how it is that you always manage to twist the argument upside down. Do you not know that this imitator, as you call him, will, if he choose, put to death the man who does not imitate him, and will take away from him all that he has?

S. I must know, good Callicles, unless I am deaf, for I have heard it over and over again of late, both from you, and from Polus, and in fact from almost everybody else in the city. But now listen to what I have to say. Kill him, he may, indeed, if he choose; but he will still be the wicked man, the other the pure and upright one.

C. And is not that just the vexatious part of it?[66]

S. Not to any one of sense, as our argument shows. Or do you think that a man ought to be planning how he may live the longest life, and cultivating those arts which are sure to save us from dangers, like, for instance, this art of rhetoric, which you bid me cultivate because it brings one safely through the law courts?

C. Yes, by Zeus, and it is good advice that I give you?

S. And how, esteemed sir, about the art of swimming; do you look upon that as a very wonderful thing?

C. Not I, by Zeus.

S. And yet that too saves men from death when they find themselves in any predicament where this art is necessary. Or if you think the example too trifling I will give you a more important one, the art of seamanship, which saves not only the lives of men but their bodies and possessions also from the uttermost dangers, just as rhetoric does. Yet for all that, it is modest and unpretentious, and does not give itself airs nor assume the attitude of having accomplished some transcendent act. But, although it brings to pass just what the art of the pleader does, it charges, I think, only two obols [66] for conveying a man hither in safety from Ægina; and as the largest price of the great service of conveying safely all that I just mentioned, a man himself and his children and possessions and womenkind, from Egypt or Pontus, and landing them in the harbour, it charges just two drachmas; and he who possesses the art in question and has effected all this gets out and walks along the seashore by the side of his ship with full modest bearing. For he knows, I presume, that he must take into account how uncertain it is which of his passengers he has benefited by not letting them be drowned and which of them he has injured, 512 being aware that they are no whit better either in body or soul when they disembark than when they went on board. And so he reasons thus: if it be true that a man with great and incurable bodily diseases who escapes drowning is wretched only in that he has not died, and has nothing to be grateful for, it cannot be that when that which is more precious than the body, — the soul, — is a prey to many and incurable diseases, he ought to go on living, and that one would do him any service in rescuing him from the sea or from the law court or from any other peril whatever. No, indeed; he knows that for the wicked man it is better not to live at all, since he must needs live ill.[67]

It is for this reason that the pilot is not wont to put on airs even though he does save our lives; no, my friend, nor the engineer either, though there are times when he is second neither to the general nor to the pilot even, nor indeed to any one at all in ability to save, for he has been known to save whole cities. You do not think him on a level with the lawyer, do you? And yet, Callicles, if he cared to talk and boast of his profession, as you others do, he might well overwhelm you with his talk, urging and enjoining upon you the duty of becoming engineers, as if nothing else were of any account; for he has plenty to say for himself. None the less, however, do you look down upon him and this art of his, and, by way of reproach, you dub him "maker of machines," and you would never consent to give your daughter in marriage to his son or to accept his daughter for yours. And yet, judging from the reasons for which you praise your own profession, what right have you to look down upon the engineer and the others I have just named?. I know you would say that you are a better man, and come of better stock. But if the better is not what I declare it to be, and if virtue consists only in saving yourself and your possessions, whatever manner of man you may be, your condemnation of the engineer and of the doctor and of all the other arts invented for safety becomes ridiculous. Nay, my good friend, but consider whether the high and noble thing be not something besides saving and being saved. Surely he who is a true man ought not to consider whether his life is to last any special time, nor indeed to love life at all; but, leaving all care of this to God, and believing with the women that no man may escape his destiny, he should examine how he may best live the time he has yet to live [68] — whether by making himself like that government under which he happens to live, just as it now behooves you to become as like the people of Athens as possible, if you would be beloved of them and acquire great power in the State. See to it, my good sir, whether this will profit you and myself as well, that we do not fare like those women of Thessaly who they say draw the moon down from heaven; [69] for the choice we make of power in the State will involve our dearest interests. But if you imagine that any mortal man can impart to you such an art as shall enable you to acquire great power in this city and yet remain unlike its governing body, whether for better or for worse, you are, Callicles, it seems to me, not rightly advised. For not only their imitator but of like nature with them must you be, if you intend to have any real friendship with the Demus of Athens or with Demus the son of Pyrilampes either, by Zeus. He, then, who will bring about the closest likeness between you and them, he it is who will make you a statesman, in the sense in which you aspire to be a statesman, and a rhetorician. For every one is delighted when words are spoken which agree with his own character, and displeased when they are of a nature foreign to it. But perhaps you are of another mind, my dear fellow. Have we anything to say about all this, Callicles?

C. I know not, Socrates, how it is that you seem to me in the right. But still I share the feeling of most men; I am not altogether convinced by what you say.

S. Because the love of Demus, Callicles, which is within your own soul stands out against me. I doubt not, however, that if we return to these questions and look into them more carefully you will be convinced.

[513 D – 515 D   Again, a contrast is drawn between the training which aims at self-gratification and has been described as a "flattery," and that which has in view the moral improvement of the person ministered to, ability to effect which is the only test of fitness for office. "For, surely, Callicles," Socrates urges, "if we two were about to assume charge of some public work, we should begin by ascertaining, one from the other, whether we had acquired a practical knowledge of the art of building and from whom, and whether any previous work undertaken by us had been successful and we ourselves were capable of assuming charge without the supervision of our masters. Or, again, if we were candidates for the office of state physician you would assuredly ask: 'And how is it with Socrates himself as to bodily health? Or is there any one else, either free man or slave, who has ever been cured of disease by Socrates?' And if the answer were to prove unsatisfactory, then, by Zeus, Callicles, it would be the very height of folly for people like ourselves, who had never before, even in private, practiced the art, to set up as public physicians, and to begin, as the saying has it, 'with the wine jar to learn the potter's art?'[70] And so now, Callicles, seeing that you yourself are entering upon public life, and seeing that you find fault with me for not doing likewise, let us each see how it is with one another. Is there any one, whether citizen or foreigner, free man or slave, who from being bad, unjust, licentious, and unrestrained, has through Callicles become good and upright?" Again Callicles tries to avoid coming to the point, and exclaims: —]

C. You are trying to pick a quarrel with me, Socrates.

S. No, I assure you I am questioning in no such spirit, but only from an earnest wish to know how you think our city ought to be administered, whether, that is, in entering upon public affairs, you intend devoting yourself to anything but to make us as good citizens as possible? Have we not several times already confessed that this is the duty of the statesman? Have we confessed it or have we not? Answer me. Very well, I will answer for you : we have. If this, then, is what it is the good man's duty to bring about in his own city, do me the favour to recall the men you mentioned a while ago, and to tell me if you still hold them to have been good citizens. I mean Pericles and Cimon and Miltiades and Themistocles.

C. I do.

S. Then if they were good, they of course, each one of them, changed their fellow citizens from worse to better. Did they do this or not?

C. They did.

S. Consequently the people of Athens, when Pericles first addressed them, were worse than when he spoke at the last?

C. Probably.

S. Not *probably* at all, esteemed sir, but *necessarily*, by our own confession; that is to say, if he was a good citizen.

C. What has that to do with it?

S. Nothing; only just tell me this, whether the Athenians are said to have been made better by Pericles, or, on the contrary, to have been corrupted by him; for I do hear that Pericles, who first instituted serving for hire, made of the Athenians a lazy, cowardly, garrulous, covetous set of men.

C. It is from the company of the bruised ears, Socrates, that you hear this.[71]

S. But I not only hear, I know for a certainty, and so do you, that in the beginning

Pericles was held in high esteem, and that the Athenians, while they were as yet worse men, found him by no means worthy of a disgraceful
516 sentence. Yet at the close of Pericles' life, after he had made them good and upright citizens, they found him guilty of fraud and came very near sentencing him to death, evidently regarding him as a sorry fellow.[72]

C. Well, what if they did? Does this make Pericles a bad man?

S. Surely a man of this sort who had charge of asses and horses and oxen would be accounted a bad guardian, if the animals when he assumed charge of them were not addicted to kicking or butting or biting, but grew so wild under his guardianship that they developed these habits; or perhaps you do not regard a man as a bad guardian of animals of any kind if, although hitherto gentle, they have become wilder under his guardianship. Do you or do you not?

C. Well, yes, to oblige you.

S. Will you oblige me further by answering me whether man is or is not one of the animals?

C. Of course he is.

S. And it was men that Pericles had under his charge, was it not?

C. Yes.

S. Well then, as we agreed just now, must they not needs have been made more just by him instead of less just, if he had cared for them as a good statesman ought?

C. Yes, of course.

S. And are not just men, as Homer said, quiet and gentle?[73] What say you? Is it not so?

C. Yes.

S. Whereas, when he had done with them they were wilder than when he took them in charge, and this towards himself, which was the last thing he could have wished.

C. Do you wish me to agree with you?

S. If you think what I say true.

C. Well, be it so.

S. And if wilder, then worse and more unjust.

C. So be it.

S. According to this view, then, Pericles was not a good statesman.

C. You say not.

S. And so do you, from all you have admitted. But tell me again about Cimon. Did not those who were under his care ostracize him, that they might not hear the sound of his voice for ten years? And did they not do the same to Themistocles, and moreover sentence him to exile? And Miltiades, the hero of Marathon, they voted to have cast into the pit, and would he not have been thrown into it, had it not been for the presiding officer?[74] And yet if these had been good men, as you say they were, they would never have suffered such things. Surely, skilful chariot-drivers do not escape a tumble from their chariots in the beginning, only to get thrown out after they have got their horses well in hand and have themselves become better drivers. That is not the way either with chariot-driving or any other employment, do you think it is?

C. No, I do not.

S. Apparently, then, what we said at first is true,—not a single man do we know who has ever been a good statesman in this city. This you admitted of men at the present day, but you denied it of a former age, and brought up these men as examples; whereas it now appears that they are but on a level with our own statesmen, so that if they really were rhetoricians it was not the true art of rhetoric that they used, no, nor the flattering kind either, or they would not have had such a fall.

C. And yet, Socrates, there is not a man of the present day who is not a long way from performing such acts as were performed by any one of these you choose to name.

S. My dear fellow, I am not blaming them, at least not as servants of the State; on the contrary, I regard them as more serviceable than those of the present day, and better able to fulfil the desires of the State. Nevertheless, in the matter of not giving way to those desires but changing the bent of them, and using force and persuasion alike, to the end that the citizens be made better, they in no wise, so to speak, differed from those of to-day; and yet this is the sole business of a good citizen. So far, indeed, as ships are concerned, and walls and harbours and all that sort of thing, they were, I grant you, more skilful in supplying these. But here we are, you and I, making a ridiculous business out of our discussion; for all the time that we talk we are always coming back again to the same point, and each misunderstanding what the other says.

[517 D – 518 A Socrates now refers again to his favourite analogy of the body and the soul. The care of the body, he declares, is of two kinds, the one ministering to and humouring its desires, as do the so-called arts of the cook, the weaver, the shoemaker; the other assuming control of these inferior and slavish arts and using them only so far as they conduce to the real good of the body, being enabled so to do from its own knowledge of their effect for good or for evil.]

S. Now when I assert that the same is true of the soul, you seem at the time to understand, and you assent as if you grasped my meaning, and then a little while after you come and tell me that our city has had good and upright citizens; and when I ask you to name them, you bring up, it seems to me, just the same kind of men as if when I had asked you who have been or who are the best trainers of the body you were to tell me, in all seriousness, that Thearion the baker, and Mithaecus who wrote the Sicilian cook-book, and Sarambus the vintner, are all three wonderful trainers of the body, because, forsooth, they understand producing, the first bread, the second fancy dishes, and the third wine.[75]

And I dare say, Callicles, you would have been offended if I had said to you : Man, you know nothing at all about gymnastics ; the fellows of whom you prate to me are but stewards and caterers to the appetites, who have no high and noble ideas concerning even these, but after they have fattened, as it may be, and stuffed men's bodies, and received praise of them, will end by making them lose even the flesh they had before. Owing to their inexperience, however, the sufferers will not attribute their diseases and the falling off of their former flesh to the feast-givers ; but those who happen to be near them and to be their advisers at some later time when this process of stuffing, carried on regardless of health, has brought disease upon them, these they will censure, and if they can, they will do them harm ; while the others, the true cause of their troubles, they will warmly praise. And you, Callicles, are doing very much the same thing now; you praise the men who have feasted our citizens and regaled them with all they desire; and every one says that it is they who have made the city great, not perceiving that through these very men of the past it has become swollen and corrupt. For, without caring for temperance and justice, they have filled the city with harbours, and docks, and walls, and tribute-money, and all such nonsense; and then when a sudden attack of disease has come upon them they fall to blaming the councillors of the day, while they praise Themistocles and Cimon and Pericles, the real authors of their troubles. And you, too, they will attack, if you do not take care, and my friend Alcibiades as well,[76] when they find themselves losing not only what they have lately acquired, but even that which they formerly possessed; and, although you were not the cause of their misfortunes, you may have helped to bring them about.

One very absurd thing withal occurs to-day, as it did amongst men of the past. When the city deals with one of these statesmen as a criminal, I notice that every one is full of protestations and complaints, for all the world as if they were suffering terrible things. "After rendering the city such good and numerous services, that their ruin should be brought about thus unjustly by her!"—such is the burden of their song. But the whole thing is false. There never yet was a guardian of a city whose ruin could be unjustly brought about by the very city which' was under his guardianship. And with the Sophists it is much the same as with those who pretend to be statesmen. For the Sophists, although clever in other respects, do this strange thing; they call themselves teachers of virtue, and yet they are always accusing their pupils of treating them unjustly, by keeping back their pay and not even returning them thanks for all the good they have done them. Now what could be more absurd than the notion that men who have been made good and just, whose injustice, indeed, has been taken away by their teacher and justice put in its place, can commit injustice by means of that which is no longer in them? Does not this strike you as absurd, my friend? Really, Callicles, by your unwillingness to answer you have forced me into making a speech.

C. And you are the man who could not talk unless he could get some one to answer him!

S. So it seems; certainly I have talked long enough on this occasion, on account of your not being willing to answer me. But tell me in the name of friendship, good sir, do you not think it unreasonable that any one should claim to have made another man good, and then, after the man has been made good by him and still continues so, should accuse him of being bad?

C. Yes, I do think so.

S. Well, do you not hear those who profess to instruct other men in virtue saying such things?

520 *C.* Yes, but why should you talk of men who are of no account?

[520 A – 521 A In reply, Socrates begs to know wherein the difference lies between the Sophists, spoken of by Callicles with such contempt, and the rhetoricians, who, after announcing that as guardians of the city they make the improvement of the citizens their chief care, proceed to disclaim all responsibility in the evil actions of their wards. Again taking up the comparison already drawn * between the sophistic and rhetorical arts, wherein the one is likened to legislative, the other to administrative justice, he declares the former to be superior to the latter in the same degree that the art of the trainer is superior to that of the physician, — the latter working only cure, the former prevention. In one respect, however, the two are identical, — both profess to take away even the capacity for injustice, whereby they differ from all the other arts. They, for example, who follow the profession of training, though they profess to impart swiftness of foot, do not pretend to increase their pupils' sense of justice, and these, therefore, do rightly in stipulating beforehand for proper recompense. But those whose profession it is to make other men just ought surely to have no

* See page 26.

doubt that those under their care will act in all things with honour and liberality.

Socrates now returns to the main question at issue and asks : —]

521   *S.* Well, to which service of the State do you invite me — define me that. Am I to play the part of the physician and exert myself to make the Athenians as good as possible, or that of a servant and minister to their pleasure? Tell me the truth, Callicles, for it is but fair that, having begun by opposing me so boldly, you should finish all that is in your mind to say. Speak out then now, freely and frankly.

C. Very well; I say that of one who will minister to them.

S. What, most high-minded sir, you invite me to become a flatterer!

C. Or a Mysian, if you prefer to call it that, Socrates;[77] for unless you do all this —

S. Now do not tell me what you have said so many times already, that any one who desires will bring about my death, lest I in my turn declare that this will be a bad man killing a good one; and do not tell me either that he will take away my possessions, if I have any, lest I declare that even if he does take them away he will get no good from them; for as he came by them unjustly, so will he use them unjustly; and if unjustly, then disgracefully; and if disgracefully, then hurtfully.

C. How confident you seem, Socrates, that you yourself will never suffer any of these things! just as if you dwelt in a world apart, and may not very likely be brought into a court of law by some wretched and good-for-nothing fellow.

S. I am a fool, Callicles, in very truth, if I do not believe that any one in this city, whosoever he be, may suffer this fate. But well I know also that if I ever appear before a court of justice and am in danger of any of the evils you name, it will be a bad man who accuses me; for no good man would accuse an innocent one. And if I were to suffer death it were no strange thing. Shall I tell you why I look for this?

C. Pray do.

S. I believe myself to be one among a very few, if not the only one of the Athenians who attempts the true art of politics, and the only man of the present day who practises statesmanship. Seeing, then, that it is not with a view to gratifying my fellow-citizens, not for their pleasure but for their good that I say what I am in the habit of saying, and seeing that I am not willing to adopt all these subtle devices which you recommend, I shall have nothing at all to say in the court of justice. It will be with me as I told Polus, — I shall be judged just as a physician would be judged if he were brought before a court of little boys on a charge preferred by a pastry cook. Only consider what such a physician would plead in his own defence before such judges, were some one to accuse him, saying : "My boys, many and great are the evils which this man has wrought upon you ; the very youngest of you he disables by means of the knife and of cautery, and drives you to extremities by parching and suffocation, 522 giving you the bitterest potions and compelling you to endure hunger and thirst ; not like myself who have feasted you upon every variety of good things." What, think you, would a physician caught in such evil plight have to say for himself? Or if he were to speak the truth and say: "All this, my boys, I did for your health's sake," what kind of clamour do you suppose such judges as these would raise? A mighty one, would they not?

C. Very likely. At least one must suppose so.

S. Do you not suppose he would be in great straits to know what to say ?

C. Of course he would.

S. And well I know that were I to appear in a court of justice, I should have just such an experience as this. For I shall have no pleasures to bring up as having provided for them, which are what they account good services and benefits, though I for my part envy neither those who provide such things nor those for whom they are provided. And if any one asserts that I ruin the young by driving them to extremities, or that I ill-treat the old by using harsh words to them, whether in private or public, there will be no use in telling him the truth, that "I am right in saying all that I do say," and that "I am working for your interest, O my judges," or in saying anything else at all.[78] So that I must, in all probability, submit myself to my fate, whatever it may be.

C. And so you think, Socrates, do you, that a man is well off who, in any city, meets with such a fate as this, and is powerless to help himself?

S. Yes, Callicles, if it be with him as you have several times admitted it is, if he has helped himself by never either speaking or doing anything unjust towards either gods or men. For this, as we have many times agreed, is the best possible help he can render himself. If, then, any one were to convict me of incapacity to render this help to myself or to another, I should be ashamed, whether I were convicted before a few or many judges or by myself alone; and if I were to die on account of this incapacity, I should be distressed. But if I were to meet my end from want of proficiency in rhetoric of the flattering kind, right sure I am that you would behold me bearing death with all cheerfulness. For the mere matter of dying no one fears, unless it be some one utterly devoid of reason and manliness; what a man fears is to act unjustly.[79] For to arrive in the world below with a load of foul deeds upon the soul is of all evils the uttermost. In proof of which, if you will permit me, I will tell you a story.

C. Well, since you have gone through the rest, you might as well finish this too.

S. Hearken, then, as the saying goes, to a right noble story. To you, I dare say, it may appear as a fairy tale, but to me it is not so, for what I am about to tell you I tell you as the truth. As Homer tells us, when Zeus and Poseidon and Pluto had inherited the dominion from their father, they divided it between themselves.[80] Now amongst the gods, there was in the time of Cronos, and has been ever since to our own day, this law in respect to men, that he who has passed his life in justice and piety shall depart, when he comes to die, to the Happy Isles, and there dwell in all blessedness, beyond the reach of ill; while he whose life has been unjust and impious shall go to the prison-house of retribution and punishment which men call Tartarus. And in the time of Cronos, nay, still later under the rule of Zeus, they who sat in judgment were alive, and those they tried were living men, for the trial took place upon the same day that it was appointed them to die; and thus the judgments were wrongly awarded. Whereupon, Pluto and the guardians of the Happy Isles went to Zeus with the complaint that the wrong men constantly found their way to either place. Then spake Zeus: "I will make an end to this," quoth he; "the judgments are now wrongly given, because when the trial takes place, they who are tried are wrapped about in their clothing; for they are tried while still alive. And there are many," he said, "whose souls are evil, and who are yet clothed in fair bodies and in pride of birth and riches, and who, moreover, at the trial produce witnesses to testify that they have lived righteous lives. Now all this imposes upon the judges, and then, too, they themselves give judgment with their clothing all about them, eyes, ears, and the whole body covering their soul as a veil; all which, namely, their own clothing and that of the persons to be judged, is a hindrance to them. In the first place, then," said he, "there must be an end to their foreknowledge of death, for now they know its approach. Wherefore I have already laid my command upon Prometheus that he make an end of this knowledge.[81] In the second place, before they are tried they must be already stripped of all these coverings; for the trial must take place after they are dead. And the judge must be stripped also and he himself be dead, his very soul looking upon the very soul of each man the instant he has died, bereft of all kinsfolk and having left behind upon the earth that glamour of which we spoke; that the sentence may be a just one. Now, I, perceiving all this before you did, have already appointed as judges my own sons, two from Asia, Minos and Rhadamanthus, and one from Europe, 524 Aeacus.[82] These, therefore, so soon as they are dead shall sit in judgment in the meadow at the three cross-roads whence lead the two paths, the one to the Happy Isles, the other to Tartarus. And those from Asia shall be judged by Rhadamanthus, those from Europe by Aeacus. But upon Minos I will confer the dignity of deciding as umpire whenever the other two are in any doubt; that the sentence which concerns the last journey of man may as far as possible be just."

This, Callicles, is what I have heard and believe to be true, and from these stories I gather some such inference as this. Death, as it seems to me, is nothing but the separation from one another of two things, the soul and the body.[83] And after their separation one from the other, each retains none the less its own nature, the same that it had when the man was yet alive, the body its own character and habits and experiences, which are all plainly to be discerned, insomuch that if the living man, whether from nature or breeding or both, had a large body, just so large is his body after he is dead; and if he was fat when alive, then after death he is fat also, and so of every other condition; or again, if he was in the habit of wearing his hair long, in death also he will have long hair.[84]

Again, if in life he was some worthless fellow whose body was scarred with stripes, traces of the scourge or of other wounds, the same are to be seen upon his body when he is dead. And if while he was yet alive his limbs were broken or distorted, all this is visible after death. In a word, whatever aspect the body presented during life, it presents the same, in most if not in all respects, for a certain time after death. Now I hold, Callicles, that the same is true of the soul. No sooner is it stripped of the body than all its qualities are made manifest, those which were a part of its nature as well as those brought about in the man's soul by the conduct of his life. Accordingly, when they arrive in the presence of the judge, those from Asia, for example, in the presence of Rhadamanthus, he places them before him and looks into each man's soul.[85] Whose it is he knows not, but oftentimes when it is the soul of the Great King or of some other monarch or potentate that he has laid hands upon, he perceives that in it there is no soundness at all, but that it is all marked by the scourge and covered with the scars that come of perjury and injustice, — the foul marks which its own evil acts have left imprinted upon the soul, — and by reason of vainglory and deceit it is crooked in every part, and because it was never trained in truth there is no straightness in it. He sees, moreover, that the soul, by reason of wantonness and license and pride and incontinence, is full of disproportion and ugliness; and beholding all this he straightway sends it off, laden with dishonour, to the place of imprisonment, where it must endure the sufferings that are its due.

Now every one who suffers punishment, if the punishment has been rightly dealt him by another, must needs either himself be made better and thus benefited thereby, or else serve as an example to others, that they, seeing the sufferings which he endures, may be made better through dread of them. And those who are benefited by receiving punishment from gods and men are they who have committed sins not past cure; nevertheless, both here and in Hades, only through pain and suffering does the benefit come to them, for there is no other way whereby they may be set free from injustice.[86] But those who have committed the greatest crimes, and who are, by reason of these, past cure, are set up as examples; and although, because they are incurable, they are no longer capable of deriving any benefit themselves, other men are benefited who behold them enduring for all time the greatest, the most grievous, and the most fearful torments, on account of their sins, hung up as warnings in the prison-house of Hades below, to serve as a spectacle and a caution to the wicked who are constantly arriving there. And I tell you that among them Archelaus too will be, if what Polus says of him is true, and likewise any other tyrant of his stamp. It seems to me, indeed, that these examples for our warning are for the most part taken from among the tyrants and kings and powerful of the earth and such as have to do with affairs of state; for these men, in virtue of their authority, commit the greatest and most unholy crimes.[87] To this Homer bears witness; for he has described those who suffer punishment for all time in the world below as kings and potentates, — like Tantalus and Sisyphus and Tityus.[88] But Thersites, on the other hand, or any other bad man who was a commoner, no one has described as visited by the direst punishments because he was incurable; for he had not, I take it, the power, and so he was more fortunate than they who had it. No, Callicles, it is amongst the powerful of the earth that the men of surpassing wickedness are found, although there is no reason why good men should not be found there too, and such as these are all worthy of admiration; for it is a hard thing, Callicles, and deserving of great praise for a man to have full power to act unjustly and yet live his life aright. Few, indeed, are the men of this stamp; but still there have been now and again, and will, I believe, yet be good and noble men who possess in its perfection this virtue of rightly dealing with whatever may have been entrusted to them.

One there is, indeed, who has gained much renown amongst all the other Greek peoples, — Aristides, the son of Lysimachus.[89] But for the most part, my friend, the powerful of the earth are found to be wicked.

As I was saying, however, Rhadamanthus, when he lays hands upon one of this sort, knows nothing further about him, neither who he is, nor what was his birth, nought indeed save that he is wicked. And when he perceives this he sends him away to Tartarus, having first set upon him a mark to show whether he is curable or past cure ; and when he has arrived there he suffers such things as he deserves. Again, Rhadamanthus sees before him a soul of another sort, the soul of a man who has lived in all truth and holiness, whether in private life or otherwise, — especially, Callicles, let me tell you, one who has lived as a philosopher and busied himself with his own affairs, not with outside matters, — and then he is well pleased, and him he sends away to the Happy Isles. In like manner does Aeacus ; and these both give judgment rod in hand ; while Minos sits apart and has the whole in charge, he alone bearing a golden sceptre, just as Odysseus in Homer speaks of seeing him : —

"Bearing a golden sceptre, and ruling o'er the dead." [90]

Now for myself, Callicles, I am persuaded of the truth of these stories, and I study how I may present my soul before the judge whole and undefiled; and so, bidding farewell to those things which most men account honours and looking onward to the Truth, I shall earnestly endeavour to grow so far as may be in goodness, and thus live, and thus, when the time comes, die.

And, to the best of my power, I exhort all other men also; and you especially, in my turn, I exhort to this life and this contest, which is, I protest, far above all contests here. And upon you I cast the reproach that you will not be able to save yourself when you come to that trial and that judgment of which I have just spoken, but when you come to appear before the judge, the son of Aegina, and he has you within his grasp, you will stand there with swimming head and open mouth, you no less there than I here, and very likely some one will strike you, yes, strike you insultingly upon the cheek, and treat you with every contumely.[91].

Now all this, I dare say, seems to you as some old nurse's tale, and you no doubt despise it; and indeed there would be nothing strange in despising it, if by dint of searching we could find aught better and truer. But here, as you see, there are three of you, the wisest of all the Greeks of to-day, yourself and Polus and Gorgias; and yet you can bring up nothing to prove that we ought to live any other life than this which is shown to be to our advantage in yonder place no less than here. And while all these other propositions of ours have been refuted, this alone remains steadfast, — that committing injustice is to be shunned rather than suffering it; and that beyond all things else a man must take heed not to *seem* but to *be* good both in private and in public;[92] and that if he become in any respect wicked he must be punished for it, because second only to *being* just is to *become* just, and through punishment to atone for sin; and that he must shun every flattery, whether it concerns himself or others, the few or the many, and must use both rhetoric and every other agency in the cause of justice alone.

Be persuaded, then, by me, and follow me to that place where, when you have reached it, you shall live in happiness both in life and after death, as our argument testifies. And let whosoever will despise you as a fool and maltreat you if he wish; yea, by Zeus, and cheerfully let him deal you that insulting blow, for no evil will come upon you if you be truly good and upright, and abide in the practice of virtue. And after we have thus practised it together, we will then, if it seems our duty, apply ourselves to the affairs of the State or whatever else we think best; then we will give counsel as being better fitted to give it than we are now. Disgraceful were it indeed for us, in the condition we now find ourselves to be in, to take upon ourselves airs as if we were of some account, when we can never hold to the same opinion upon the same questions, though they be of the greatest importance; such is the depth of our ignorance! Let us, therefore, use the present argument as a guide which points out to us that the best way of life is to practise justice and every other virtue, and so to live and so to die. This way, then, we will follow, and we will call upon all other men to do the same, not that which you believe in and call upon me to follow; for that way, Callicles, is nothing worth.

THE REPUBLIC.

THE REPUBLIC.

BOOK VII.

In the book which precedes this, Socrates maintains that only by living the life of a philosopher can a knowledge of the intellectual world, where alone true being resides, be gained. The supreme idea of this higher world, the ideal form of Good, whose light illumines all other ideas in the intellectual world, he likens to the sun, whose light must illumine any object which the eye would see clearly in the visible world. The thought is carried out in the following allegory of a cave or lower world, which bears the same relation to the visible world in which we live that the latter bears to the world of pure ideas above it.

The conversation is between Socrates and Glaucon, Socrates speaking in the first person.

514 "PICTURE to yourself a company of men in a kind of underground cavern-like dwelling, which has an opening towards the light extending all the way across one side; here from childhood they have been fastened by the legs and the neck, in such wise that they are kept ever in one position and see only what is in front of them, because by reason of the chains they cannot turn their heads round. Light, how-

ever, they have from a fire which is burning high up at some distance behind them; and between the fire and the prisoners there runs a raised road, along which you see a low wall built like the screens which the jugglers set up between themselves and their audience, over which to display their shows." [98]

"I see it all," said Glaucon.

"Imagine, furthermore, men who are carrying behind this wall images of men and all sorts of animals, made of wood and stone and wrought in every fashion, and other articles of every kind, which project above the wall; and suppose, as would be natural, that some of those who carry the images are talking, others silent."

"This is a strange picture," said he, "and strange prisoners are these."

"Very like ourselves," I rejoined. "Do you suppose, in the first place, that people in such case could ever see anything, whether of themselves or of each other, save the shadows which the fire casts upon the side of the cave directly opposite them?"

"How could they," he answered, "if all their lives they had been forced to keep their heads immovable?"

"And what of the objects which are carried past? Would it not be the same thing with these?"

"Naturally it would."

"And if they could talk together, do you not

believe that they would agree upon common names for the figures they saw passing before them?"

"Necessarily they would."

"And how about this. If there were an echo from the prison wall in front of them, do you believe that whenever one of the passers-by spoke, they would suppose the sound to come from anything but the passing shadow?"

"No, indeed, I do not," was his reply.

"So that, in fact," said I, "people of this sort would hold nothing for real, save the shadows of the images."

"Necessarily so."

"Consider then," I continued, "what would be the effect of their release from prison and cure from folly if it came about thus. Suppose that one of them were set free and forced all of a sudden to get up and turn his head round, and walk and look up toward the light, and suppose it pained him to do all this, and he was unable, on account of the brightness, to look at the objects of which all along he had been seeing the shadows. What, think you, would he say if some one told him that what he had been seeing all along was an illusion, but that now, from being somewhat nearer to reality and turned towards things more real, he saw more truly; and if moreover each passing object were pointed out to him, and he were forced to answer and say what each one was?

Do you not suppose he would be bewildered, and deem what he had been used to see far more real than what was now pointed out to him?"

"Much more real," he said.

"And if he were forced to look at the light itself, would not his eyes pain him, and would he not turn away and again take refuge in such things as he was able to look upon, and believe that these were in reality more distinct than those now pointed out?"

"Yes, so it would be," he said.

"Now suppose some one were to drag him by force up the rough steep ascent, and not let him go until he had been drawn out into the light of the sun, would he not, while he was being dragged along, suffer pain and distress, and on coming into the sunlight, would not his eyes be so filled with its brilliancy that he would be unable to see a single one of the things which we now call real?"

"Yes, indeed," he said, "in the first moment at least."

"Yes, he would certainly need to get accustomed to the upper world if he is ever to discern objects there. And first he would find it easier to distinguish the shadows, then the reflections in water of men and other objects, and after that the objects themselves. And from these he would turn his gaze upon the light of the stars and of the moon, finding it easier to look at things in the heavens and the heavens themselves by night, than at the sun and the light of the sun by day."

"How could it be otherwise?"

"And last of all, I suppose, he would look upon the sun, not its mere image reflected in water or in some other foreign substance, but the sun itself in its own abode, beholding it as it really is."

"Undoubtedly he would."

"And this would lead him to reflect that the sun it is which orders the seasons and the years, and is guardian of all things in the visible world, and in some way the cause of those things that he and his fellows have been wont to see."

"It is plain," he assented, "that the one step would lead to the other."

"Well then, calling to mind his former abode and his whilom wisdom and his fellow-prisoners, do you not think he would deem himself blessed in the change, and pity them?"

"Indeed I do."

"And suppose it were their habit among themselves to bestow praises and honours and rewards upon him whose vision was keenest for the passing objects, and who best remembered which of them were wont to pass first and which last and which together, and was therefore best able to foretell what was coming next, would he, think you, be eager for these praises and envious of those who are vested with high honour and authority among them; or would he not rather feel, with Homer, that he would infinitely prefer to be —

'Bound to the soil, and serve another man, though portionless,'⁹⁴

and suffer any manner of thing, rather than go on holding those opinions and living in that way?"

"Yes," said he, "I believe he would suffer anything rather than go on living in that way."

"And now consider this, too," I said; "suppose a man of this sort were to return below and seat himself in his old place, would not his eyes, coming thus suddenly out of the sunlight, be filled with darkness?"

"Most certainly they would."

"And if he had once more to enter into a contest with those who had always remained prisoners, in discerning the shadows we have spoken of, his sight being as yet weak and his eyes not having yet adjusted themselves to the new conditions, and if it should take no little time to get used to these, would they not laugh him to scorn, and declare that his visit to the upper world had spoiled his eyes for him, and that the ascent was not worth even the attempt? And if any one tried to release them and lead them upwards, they would put him to death if they could manage to get him into their clutches; would they not?"

"That they would," said he.

"Here, then, my dear Glaucon," I said, "you have the parable which must be added to what we spoke of before. The world seen by the eye is represented by the prison house, the light of the fire by the power of the sun; and if you will take the upward journey and the sight of things above to be the ascent of the soul to the world of thought, you will not fail to apprehend my hope, since you wish to know it, though whether or not it be true God only knows. My belief then is this: in the realm of knowledge the Idea of Good is the final goal and is perceived only with effort, but when once perceived it is recognized as the source of all things true and beautiful, in the visible world giving birth to light and the lord of light,[95] in the world of thought standing forth itself as the dispenser of truth and reason; and upon this his gaze must be bent who would act rationally whether in private or in public."

"I agree with you," he rejoined, "so far, at least, as I am able to follow."

"Pray, then," said I, "agree with me also in thinking it no marvel that they who have attained this height do not desire to take part in the affairs of men; but their souls ever impel them to linger above; for this were but natural, if our parable may still be applied."

"Quite natural," he said.

"Well, then, is it strange, do you think, that a man who passes from contemplation of the divine to the human, conducts himself awkwardly and makes a very ridiculous appearance if he is compelled, while his sight is still weak and he is not yet thoroughly accustomed to the darkness around him, to enter into a contest, in a court of justice or elsewhere, concerning shadows of justice or rather the images which cast these shadows, and to dispute about the notions entertained concerning these by men who have never had a glimpse of justice herself?" [96]

"Not strange in the least," he replied.

518 "On the contrary," I added, "if a man has any sense, he will remember that there are two kinds of disturbance of the eyes, which arise from two causes, the passage from light into darkness and the passage from darkness into light. Wherefore, reflecting that it is the same with the soul, he will not thoughtlessly laugh when he beholds one which is bewildered and unable to see clearly, but will examine whether it has come out of a brighter life and is blinded from being unaccustomed to darkness, or whether, having come out of a lower state of ignorance into a brighter life, it is dazzled by the more brilliant radiance; and then he will account the one happy in its condition and mode of life, and pity the other; and if he have a mind to laugh at this soul, his laughter will be less ridiculous than when it is directed against the soul which has come down from the light above."

"You speak most sensibly," he said.

"If this, then," I said, "is the truth in regard to these matters, we ought to believe that education is not what certain of those who profess it proclaim. For they say that they can put into the soul a knowledge which it does not possess, as if they would put sight into blind eyes." [97]

"Yes, they say they can do this," he said.

"But our argument," I continued, "makes it clear that every man has within his soul this faculty and the instrument whereby each man may acquire knowledge; and that just as we might suppose it to be impossible for the eye to turn from darkness to light save with the whole body also, so it is necessary that not this faculty only but the whole soul with it be turned round from the world of change, until it becomes able to bear the sight of the real and what is brightest in the real. And this we call the Good, do we not?"

"Yes."

"And the art would consist in bringing about in the easiest and most efficacious way this very process of conversion; not creating sight within a man, but assuming that sight is already there, only not rightly directed nor looking where it should, and contriving a remedy for this."

"I suppose so," he said.

"Now the other so-called virtues of the soul

are very like those of the body, having, as a matter of fact, no existence there in the beginning, but being afterwards engendered by custom and practice; whereas the virtue of wisdom is a part of something, it would seem, far more divine, having within itself a force which never perishes, but by the process of conversion becomes either useful and beneficent, or else useless and productive of harm. Take one of that class known for bad men, yet clever. Have you never observed what keen glances the sorry soul of the fellow darts out, and how quick he is to discern all to which his attention is turned, thus showing that his sight is not defective, but that he is impelled to use it in the service of evil, so that the more keenly he sees, so much more the harm he works?"

"Most true."

"Now then," I said, "if a soul endowed with such a nature had from childhood been shorn of all things akin to the temporal, which, like leaden weights, cling to pleasures of the table and gluttonous delights of that nature, and which turn the eye of the soul towards things below; [98] if, released from these, it had been turned towards the Truth, this self-same faculty of these self-same men would have been just as keen to discern this as to see that upon which its gaze is now directed."

"Very probably," he said.

"Then is it not also probable, nay, from

what was said before, positive, that neither those who are uneducated and unacquainted with Truth, nor those who are suffered to spend their whole life over their education, are qualified to be guardians of a state; the former because they have no single aim in life with a view to which all their actions, both private and public, are performed, the latter because of their own free will they perform no duties at all, imagining themselves, although still in the flesh, to be already dwelling far away in the Happy Isles?"

"Very true," said he.

"Our business, then, as founders of the State," said I, "is to compel the best endowed natures amongst us to reach that knowledge which we have already declared to be the highest of all, and to behold the Good and to make the upward journey of which we spoke; but when they have made the journey and have gazed their fill, we must not allow them to do what is now allowed them."

"What is that, pray?"

"To remain there," I said, "and refuse to come down again to the prisoners of whom we have been speaking, and to share in their labours and honours, whether trivial or important."

"What," he cried, "shall we act so unfairly by them, as to make them live a less desirable life when they might have a better one?"

"Again, my friend," said I, "you have forgotten that the law does not concern itself for the special welfare of any one class in the State, but strives to bring about the welfare of the whole State, binding the citizens together both by persuasion and by force, and making them sharers one with the other in the benefits which they are severally able to render for the common weal; and that it creates men of this stamp in the State, not to the end that they may be free each to betake himself wheresoever he will, but that they may be made use of for the binding together of the State."

"True," said he, "I had quite forgotten."

"Consider then, dear Glaucon," I said, "that in persuading those of us who are philosophers to have a care for others and to watch over them, we shall not be dealing unjustly by them but shall be telling them what is right. For we shall tell them that in other cities it is reasonable that men of their sort should not share in the toils of state, for they grow up of themselves, against the desire of the government, and it is right that what is of natural growth and owes its nurture to none should pay to none a nurse's wage. But you, on the other hand, we have called into existence both for your own good and for that of the whole State, to be, as it were, leaders and monarchs of the hive, because, being better and more thoroughly instructed than the others, you are better qualified to take part in life, both public and private.[89] You must, therefore, every one in his turn, go down to the abode of the others, and accustom yourselves to looking upon the darkness, for when you are once accustomed to it you will see ten thousand times better than those below, and will know what the different images are and of what they are the images, because you have beheld the truth in regard to the Beautiful and the Just and the Good. And thus shall our State be peopled; as a reality, not as a dream like most of our States, which are peopled by men fighting with one another for shadows and disputing about bearing rule, as if that were some mighty good. But the truth is, I imagine, that the State wherein those destined to rule are least eager for rule must needs be governed in the best and most peaceable way, while in the State where the rulers are of the opposite mind the opposite is true."

"Most assuredly," he said.

"And when our wards hear this, will they disobey us, and desire, not to share each in his turn the toils of state, but to pass the greater part of their time together in the world of pure thought?"

"Impossible," said he, "for our demands are just, and they are just men of whom we make them. Rather will each of them go to his post of command, as under stress of necessity, not at all like those who now bear rule in every one of our States."

"This then, my friend," I said, "is the truth of the case. If for those who are destined to rule you will seek out a life which is better than ruling, it will be possible for you to have a well-ordered State; for in such a State alone will they bear rule who are truly rich, not in gold, but in that wealth which the happy man must needs possess, — a wise and virtuous life."

NOTES.

NOTES ON THE GORGIAS.

NOTE 1, p. 1.

" To the latter end of a fray and the beginning of a feast
Fits a dull fighter and a keen guest,"
— *Henry IV.*, Part 1, Act iv. Scene 2.
is Shakespeare's paraphrase of the old saw " First at a feast and last at a fray," some version of which was evidently familiar to the contemporaries of Socrates.

According to Demosthenes (*Phil.* I. 35), this reproach was peculiarly applicable to his fellow countrymen. " Your festivals," he complains, "are always celebrated at the proper time, but as to your fleets, they always arrive too late."

NOTE 2, p. 2.

Unless Gorgias and the newcomers may be supposed to have exchanged the customary greetings before the opening words of Callicles, an interval must be imagined at this juncture, during which they take place, the dialogue being resumed with the words : " Tell me, Gorgias."

NOTE 3, p. 3.

This HERODICUS, of Leontini in Sicily, is not to be confounded with his namesake of Selymbria mentioned in the *Protagoras* (316 E), as well as in the *Republic* (406 A-B).

NOTE 4, p. 3.

The " brother of Aristophon " is no other than the celebrated Polygnotus, the painter of historical pictures, among the most noted of which were those that decorated the Lesche or assembly room attached to the temple at Delphi, representing the capture of Troy and the descent of Odysseus into Hades. This painter seems to have created a revolution in the art of his day by his success in the portrayal of character. Aristotle advises the young to study his works because they "express moral ideas" (*Pol.* VI. 5, p. 1340 a), and speaks of him as a "good character painter" in contrast to Zeuxis, whose paintings "contain nothing of character."—*Poetics*, 6, p. 1450 a. It may be conceived that Aristotle, in naming him thus, means that inasmuch as, like the best tragic poets, he conceives actions to be the results not of outside circumstances, but of character, he effects like them, "through fear and pity, purification from the passions." —*Poetics*, 6, p. 1449 b.

NOTE 5, p. 4.

Polus here quotes from his own treatise upon rhetoric, which Socrates presently speaks of having recently read (p. 22). From the general reputation of Polus, as well as from this specimen of his style, we may take it to have been an exaggeration of that of Gorgias, overladen with antitheses and filled with "jingle of sounds," which latter peculiarity Socrates subsequently parodies in addressing him as "Most polished Polus" (p. 29).

"What shall we say," it is elsewhere asked, "of Polus's school of language with its repetitions and sententious sayings and figures of speech, and the nomenclature which Licymnius bequeathed him for the purpose of forming eloquence?"—*Phaedrus*, 267 C.

NOTE 6, p. 4.

Nothing could differ more widely, both in purpose and method, than the type of rhetoric which Plato calls a "barren pastime," and "the act of inveigling men's souls with words" (*Phaedrus*, 260–261), from that "far nobler work of the dialectician who, taking a kindred soul, understands how to implant and engraft upon it words which . . . are not unfruitful, but contain within them seeds from which others again being implanted, this in one nature, that in another, the seed becomes forever undying, and the possessor of it as happy as it is in the power of man to be." — *Phaedrus*, 277 A.

NOTE 7, p. 5.

"Such is my race, and such the blood I boast."
— *Iliad*, vi. 211.

is a favourite vaunt of the Homeric heroes.

NOTE 8, p. 8.

The SCOLIA— convivial songs containing exhortations to wine, mirth, and love, and sometimes praises of gods and heroes or moral precepts and reflections — are said to have derived their name "crosswise" from the direction in which each performer in turn passed to his successor the myrtle branch held in the hand while singing. These songs, though often well-known couplets by poets such as Alcæus or Anacreon, were not unfrequently improvised upon the occasion of some banquet, which was thus converted into a contest of poetic skill, a prize being awarded at its close to the best singer.

NOTE 9, p. 8.

The scolion in question, ascribed to Epicharmus or Simonides, runs thus : —

> Best gift to mortal man is health,
> Next ranks the power which beauty lends,
> Third blameless riches to enjoy,
> Fourth to live happy days with friends.

Very similar to this was the famous couplet inscribed over the gateway of the temple of Leto at Delos, which is quoted by Aristotle (*Eth. Nicom.*, i. 8) : —

> Pure justice is most fair; best good is health;
> But sweetest far to gain what we desire.

This is found with slight changes in *Theognis*, 255, 256; and in the *Creusa* of Sophocles (*Frag.*, 328), quoted by Stobaeus (*Flor.*, 103, 15).

NOTE 10, p. 10.

ZEUXIS was a contemporary of Socrates. A native of Heraclea, in lower Italy, and a pupil of the celebrated Apollodorus, he was, like his master, more noted for the happy distribution of light and colour and the expression of transitory emotions, than for the expressive delineation of character wherein his predecessor Polygnotus excelled. To his mind, illusion was the highest quality of art, as shown by the story of the contest with Parrhasius, in which he confessed himself defeated, because, while birds had been deceived by his own painting of a cluster of grapes, his rival's skilful representation of a curtain had deceived men. Various stories are told of the high estimation set by himself upon his works. Underneath his picture of the *Athlete* he caused the inscription to be placed that it was easier to criticise than to imitate it, and when reproached for working slowly, he replied that he painted for eternity. Notwithstanding his customary charge of an admission fee to his studio, he is said, after having made a large fortune by decorating the palace of Archelaus of Macedonia, to have given his pictures away, declaring that no money was an equivalent for their value.

NOTE 11, p. 13.

About 458 B. C. the Athenians built the two original " Long Walls," probably in accordance with the former plan of Themistocles. One ran southwesterly to the newly fortified harbour of Piraeus, the other more southerly to the old roadstead at Phalerum. — *Thucyd.* i. 107, 108. Several years later, Pericles built a second wall to Piraeus, parallel to the first, so as to protect on both sides a road to the harbour. This was called the Middle Wall, as it ran between the older Piraic wall and the Phaleric wall. The two Piraic walls were sometimes called Northern and Southern, from their positions.

The walls of the city of Athens, to which Gorgias refers, were built under the direction of Themistocles himself, and were a monument of his craft and diplomatic skill. At the close of the Persian war, under the pretext that fortified towns might be useful to invaders, but in reality out of jealousy to Athens, the Lacedaemonians proposed to allow no fortifications outside the Peloponnesus. Upon this, by advice of Themistocles, the Athenians proceeded to rebuild their walls, while an embassy, headed by Themistocles himself, was sent to Sparta, ostensibly for purposes of consultation, but in reality to lengthen out the time necessary for their erection. Tidings being subsequently received in Sparta of the work going on at Athens, Lacedaemonian envoys were despatched there to learn the truth of the story, but not before a secret message had been sent by Themistocles to have them detained until his own return, which, upon the completion of the walls, he safely accomplished.

NOTE 12, p. 14.

The study of medicine was held in high honour in Greece, where it partook indeed almost of a sacred character, a solemn oath being required before pupils were admitted to the Temple of Aesculapius, the nearest approach to a medical college in that day. Many of the cities appointed public physicians, who received a regular salary from the state for their medical attendance upon the citizens, while those of their assistants who by dint of observation and natural quickness had picked up some knowledge of the healing art were deputed to minister to the slaves. In the *Laws*, a contrast is drawn between the practice of the freeman's physician and that of the slave doctor; the former proceeding from his own close observation, and from the information that he is careful to elicit from the patient or his friends, whose assent and confidence indeed is a necessary condition of the treatment; the latter exchanging never a word with the sick man or his family, but prescribing, "as if he knew all about it," whatever experimental treatment strikes his fancy, and then "bustling off full of complacent assurance to some other patient." — *Laws*, 720 C-D.

NOTE 13, p. 14.

While the gymnasia were frequented at will by those who wished to practise running, jumping, and other feats of skill, as well as boxing and wrestling, the exercises at the PALAESTRA were directed by paid instructors and confined more or less to those of a purely combative nature.

NOTE 14, p. 16.

The same "spirit of strife" is elsewhere alluded to as actuating the uneducated, who, "when they differ upon some subject, give never a thought to the truth of the matter, but are bent only upon getting their audience to agree with what they assert." — *Phaedo*, 91 A. And in still another passage this class is characterized as "incapable of subdividing a subject and examining it under its several heads, but always seeking out some verbal contradiction, so that, while imagining themselves to be engaged in discussion, they are in reality disputing." — *Repub.* 454 A.

NOTE 15, p. 19.

That knowledge is identical with right conduct was a cardinal doctrine with Socrates, who declares that since all men, so far as possible, make choice of and practise whatever seems to themselves most profitable, it can be only through lack of knowledge that they ever err in the choice of pleasures. — *Prot.* 357 D. It is, however, not in this but in its ordinary acceptation that Gorgias has spoken of knowledge throughout the whole of the preceding conversation, and it is a proof of the singular want of readiness which in general distinguishes the interlocutors of Socrates that Gorgias allows this sudden introduction of an individual and peculiar definition to pass unchallenged. Nor can we wonder that Callicles, smarting under the recollection of this undue advantage gained by Socrates, should complain, as he afterwards does, that he twists meanings to suit himself (p. 53).

It is interesting to compare with this cardinal doctrine of Socrates concerning knowledge and virtue, the opinion so strenuously insisted upon by Carlyle, that vice, or even untrue opinion, is incompatible with great intellectual power. "Believe not," he says, in speaking of Goethe, "that a great mind can be joined with a bad heart."

NOTE 16, p. 19.

This is possibly a reference, like that on page 51, to Anubis, the Egyptian deity, who is always represented with the head of a dog. What influence, if any, was exerted by Egypt upon the religious conceptions of the Greeks, it is impossible to ascertain. It is certain, however, that there are similarities between the worship of Isis and Osiris, and that of Demeter and Dionysus, and it has even been conjectured, from allusions in Plato's dialogues, that through intercourse with the Egyptian priests he had obtained the key to that mysterious and occult knowledge which the adepts of India still claim to possess.

NOTE 17, p. 22.

In defining rhetoric as "a kind of dexterity," Socrates marks the difference between the art of dialectics, which "like a coping stone crowns the other sciences" (*Repub.* 534 E), and which proceeds by the scientific method of proving by argument, and that of rhetoric itself, which, seeking only to "win men's souls by words," is in reality, like fancy cookery, "not art at all," but rather "a barren pastime." — *Phaedr.* 260–261.

The treatise on rhetoric mentioned immediately above is the same which Polus himself had previously quoted (p. 4).

NOTE 18, p. 23.

The art of "flattery," which Plato apparently regards as the faculty of securing one's own end by pandering to others, is in another dialogue described as follows: —

" The art which the mercenary has of making himself agreeable in his intercourse with others and preparing for them the bait of enjoyment, exacting as pay for his flattery nothing but his maintenance — this we should, I imagine, all of us, call a species of sweetening art." — *Sophist*, 222 E.

The art of "personal adornment" necessarily includes not only wearing fine clothes, but painting the face, dyeing the hair, and in fact all the artifices of the toilet.

Note 19, p. 24.

That the "political art" should have been held by Aristotle to embrace not only legislative justice but ethics as well, throws light upon what he considered the relative position of private and public virtue. The citizen's relation to the state outweighed all ties of kinship; compared to the public good that of the individual sank into insignificance, or rather was comprehended in the larger term of welfare of the state. In view of this there could be no greater reproach than that of having counterfeited the political art, the very embodiment of interests the loftiest and most sacred.

Note 20, p. 24.

The allusion to a "colt," the translation of Polus's name, is not unprovoked, since he has just given proof of his immaturity of mind, by demanding a panegyric of rhetoric before a proper definition of rhetoric itself has been reached.

Note 21, p. 26.

This passage may be compared with another where Socrates contrasts the Sophist and the rhetorician, to the great advantage of the former (p. 106).

Note 22, p. 26.

Anaxagoras found the key to the construction of the universe in a divine intelligence which, although not the creator of matter, had yet brought matter from its original condition of indiscriminate confusion and chaos into order and shapeliness.

Pericles was a pupil of Anaxagoras, and is said by Plato to have owed in great measure to his master his success in public life, inasmuch as from the knowledge gained from him of the higher philosophy, comprising a familiar acquaintance with the "nature of mind and matter," were derived the lofty conceptions which formed the mainspring of many of his public actions.—*Phaedrus*, 270 A.

Note 23, p. 27.

In general the "tyrant" was some ambitious noble who in times of political excitement persuaded the people to choose him as their champion against the governing body, and ended by usurping the power for himself, the originator of such a scheme having an additional chance of success, when, as in the case of Peisistratus, a descendant of Codrus, he happened to have one of the ancient kings as ancestor.

The modern use of the word tyrant has somewhat obscured its original meaning, which is that of a despotic, but not necessarily harsh or unbeneficent ruler. Deeply rooted, however, in the Greek, and especially in the Athenian mind, was a hatred of unconstitutional rule — a conviction that a government is directly answerable to the whole body of citizens, and that, this obligation once removed, it degenerates into the arbitrary and irresponsible sway of a single individual. "Tyranny," Aristotle declares, "being a compound of extreme oligarchy and democracy, is of all governments the most prejudicial to subjects, as being composed of two evils and containing in itself the perversions and errors of both these polities." — *Pol.* V. 10, p. 1310 b.

Note 24, p. 28.

The blank which occurs here does not necessarily imply the omission of some word too strong for polite ears, but more probably indicates a momentary lapse of memory such as is often filled out with some such ejaculation as "What do you call him?" or "What is his name?"

Note 25, p. 29.

A previous speech of Polus (p. 4) exemplifies the jingle of sounds for which he was celebrated, and which Socrates playfully imitates in addressing him thus.

Note 26, p. 33.

During the latter part of the Peloponnesian war, when the Athenian fleet, crippled by recent disasters, was maintaining a desperate struggle against the Lacedaemonians at Samos, a small party of the oligarchical faction contrived to wrest the power from the democracy and to establish despotic rule. The allusion in the text refers to the culminating act of the four hundred, as this party were called, when "with concealed daggers" they entered the Senate house and disbanded the five hundred senators, handing to each one, as he passed out, his pay for the remainder of the yearly term of office. The government of these self-constituted rulers was within a year broken up by internal factions, instigated probably by Theramenes, one of their own number, and democratic rule was restored.

NOTE 27, p. 35.

Notwithstanding the evil deeds of ARCHELAUS, he is highly commended by Thucydides (2. 100), who declares that he improved Macedonia to a greater extent than any one of his predecessors had done. At his court, to which Socrates is said to have been invited, Greek authors of distinction were hospitably entertained, notably Euripides, who there ended his days.

NOTE 28, p. 36.

That Plato expressly includes women with men in this passage is an indication of his views in regard to their position and responsibilities, which he expresses still more clearly in his plans for the ideal state. Denying that one kind of education will make a good guardian of a man, and another a good guardian of a woman, he insists that "in the administration of a state there are no pursuits which devolve especially upon a woman as a woman, or upon a man as a man; for natural endowments are scattered equally amongst both sexes, and a woman is by nature fitted to bear her share in every kind of pursuit just as a man is, save that in everything woman has less strength than man." And the conclusion he arrives at is that "there is no better thing for a state than that its women and its men alike be as good as possible." — *Repub.* 455–456.

Note 29, p. 38.

NICIAS is the unfortunate general whose want of energy and decision caused the destruction of the Athenian fleet before Syracuse in the Peloponnesian war; ARISTOCRATES, one of the generals sentenced to death for their failure to pick up the dead bodies of their comrades after the sea fight of Arginusae at a later period of the same war. Neither of these men can be taken as examples of inordinate greed for power or riches, and are apparently named only on the general supposition that they who possess wealth and worldly position hold these in exaggerated estimation, or possibly because their dedication of votive offerings in commemoration of successful services rendered to the state (see Note 35) may imply an undue value placed upon memorials of worldly triumph.

The offerings here alluded to were tripods, which, bearing inscribed upon them the name of the tribe to which the victor belonged, were placed upon pedestals in the neighborhood of the great theatre of Dionysus.

Note 30, p. 41.

The punishment of burning an offender alive after placing him in a sack smeared with pitch, was enforced not by legal enactment, but by mob-law. — *Repub.* 361 E.

Note 31, p. 41.

The word here translated by "bugbear" is derived from *mormo*, a hobgoblin, apparently not unlike the French *croque-mitaine*, which was held up as a terror to children. The same " bugbear terrors which are used to frighten us like children," are mentioned also in the *Crito* (46 C).

Note 32, p. 42.

Such was the public indignation roused against the generals commanding in the sea fight of the Arginusae, in consequence of their failure to pick up the dead bodies of their comrades and to render them the customary funeral rites, that it was proposed at Athens to decide upon the guilt of the offenders, not by individual trial in a court of law, before the dikasts or jurymen, but collectively and by vote of the several tribes on the occasion of a public assembly. To Socrates, as chairman of the presiding tribe, fell the duty of putting this illegal proposition to the vote, and it is his spirited refusal to do so which he now ironically ascribes to his ignorance of the proper mode of procedure.

NOTE 33, p. 49.

This is of course a playful presentation of the question, for, in opposition to a commonly received code of morals, Socrates held that "it can never be right to do another harm." — *Repub.* 335 E. Here, however, he assumes for the moment that the opposite course is right, in order to bring out his own deep conviction, that what is commonly held to be man's advantage is that which in reality often works him the greatest injury.

"The wisdom of the world is foolishness with God."— *1 Cor.* iii. 19.

NOTE 34, p. 50.

The name of PYRILAMPES, the father of DEMUS and friend of Pericles, figures in several embassies to Asia, where the physical beauty for which he was celebrated is said to have excited much admiration. But he was still better known from his cultivation of the peacock, a bird but lately introduced into Greece and still so great a rarity that visitors travelled even from Thessaly and Sparta to be present on the day of the month set apart for its exhibition to the public. It would appear that Demus had inherited his father's good looks, for he figures in the *Wasps* of Aristophanes (*vs.* 98), as a petted favourite. The coincidence of his name (Demus = people) gives Socrates an opportunity to emphasize in a natural way his disapproval of the orators for following as they did the will of the masses, instead of attempting to guide and control them.

In point of fact, the intimacy of Alcibiades with Socrates had ceased with his own advancement to political power, as a means, perhaps, towards acquiring which he had sought the society of the great master of dialectics. — *Mem.* I. ii. 17.

Note 35, p. 51.

Socrates here alludes to the Choregia, one of the so-called liturgies or public services which every citizen possessed of a certain competency was expected in his turn to render the state. The Choregus was responsible for the choruses in the public plays, his duties including not only the payment of the teachers and actors but their maintenance, and also all arrangements necessary to the performance. Another of the liturgies had for its object the training and maintenance of combatants in the public festivals and was performed by the Gymnasiarchy; and yet another, which provided the triremes or ships of war, devolved upon the Trierarchy. So heavy were the expenses sometimes incurred, that in times of great depression two citizens were allowed to share them, while on the other hand the offices were often coveted by the wealthy and ambitious, who, if the result of their endeavours was acceptable to the state, were awarded public honours, to commemorate which, tripods such as those mentioned in Note 29 were erected.

Note 36, p. 55.

It was customary for wealthy citizens to keep as pets beasts of prey, who, from having been tamed when young, had lost their savage instincts.

Note 37, p. 55.

The position taken by Callicles is the same as that of Thrasymachus in the *Republic*, who pronounces justice to be "nothing more than the interest of the stronger."—*Repub.* 338 C. The quotation from Pindar is thus paraphrased by Thompson in his edition of the *Gorgias* (1871): —

"There is a law of nature, the law of the strongest, to which all in heaven and earth must submit, and which overrides at times all positive enactments, fortifying deeds of violence which are condemned by human codes. This law sanctioned many of the exploits of Hercules, otherwise indefensible, as in particular that in which he seized, without money paid or leave asked, the cows of Geryones, and drove them from the far west away to the palace of Eurystheus at Argos."

The phrase "Law is king of all" soon passed into a proverb, and, singularly enough, came to be quoted in the sense of tyranny of convention, exactly the opposite meaning from the original one of Pindar. According to the view of Gorgias and his school, that nothing has real existence, the law of conscience would naturally be regarded in the light of a useless restraint, or perhaps even, in the words of Callicles, as a "vulgar and fallacious notion." They, on the other hand, who hold that there is an absolute and eternal Truth, have in reverence those "unwritten laws" which are acknowledged by every human conscience alive to a sense of its own responsibility. "These," Socrates held, "were appointed by the gods for men, and such as transgress these laws appointed by the gods shall suffer for it, for no man may by any possibility escape the punishment of such transgression." — XEN. *Mem.* IV., iv. 21.

NOTE 38, p. 56.

It is a significant fact that the phrase here used, καλὸν κἀγαθόν, literally "good and fair," originally a credential of gentle birth and subsequently used by Socrates as a term of the highest moral commendation, becomes upon the lips of Callicles the synonym for worldly success, a definition characteristic of the practical man in a narrow sense, to whom all occupations which have not a strictly utilitarian purpose are but foolishness. Even Isocrates, a rhetorician respected and commended by Plato himself, inveighs against the folly of grown men in pursuing philosophical studies "good only to keep very young men out of mischief," and adds that many of those "best versed in such studies are yet in the common affairs of life more ignorant than are their own pupils, not to say their household slaves." — *Panathenaicus*, p. 230 C–D. This animadversion against philosophy, as unfitting young men for public life and thus bringing about their political ruin, explains in a measure the charge brought against Socrates of corrupting the young.

NOTE 39, p. 58.

The allusion is to a passage in the *Iliad*, where the venerable Phœnix, in attempting to dissuade Achilles from his rash resolve to abandon the Greek hosts before Troy, speaks thus :

> " How, then, dear boy, can I remain behind,
> Alone ? whom with thee aged Peleus sent,
> That day when he in Agamemnon's cause
> From Phthia sent thee, inexperienc'd yet
> In all the duties of confed'rate war,
> And sage debate, on which attends renown."
> — *Iliad*, 9, 441. [Lord Derby's translation.

NOTE 40, p. 58.

These words, and also the lines on p. 56, are from the *Antiope*, one of the lost tragedies of Euripides, of which only about one hundred and twenty lines remain. The story was that AMPHION and ZETHUS, sons of Antiope by Zeus, were in their infancy confided by their mother to the care of a shepherd on Mt. Cithaeron. Zethus, who had adopted the profession of herdsman and hunter, thus reproaches his brother because, endowed by Hermes with the lyre, he has given himself up to the pursuit of music, to the neglect of practical pursuits.

> " Thou shunnest, Amphion, what thou should'st pursue,
> The nobly gifted soul which nature gave thee
> Disguising that by womanish disguise.
> No voice hast thou when justice holds her council,
> No words of weight persuasive canst thou find,
> Nor prompt in injured innocence' defence,
> The gallant counsel and the high resolve."
> — *Gorgias*. [E. Cope's translation.

NOTE 41, p. 59.

The outlaw was visited with civil death. Having no existence in the eyes of the law, he was excluded from its benefits, and thus any indignity, even this last of all insults to a Greek, — a box on the ear, — might be inflicted upon him with impunity.

NOTE 42, p. 59.

The lines from which this expression is taken are the continuation of those already quoted (p. 56), from the tragedy of *Antiope* : —

> Cease from this strain, use melody of arms,
> Song such as this shall bring thee fair renown,
> Delve, till the soil, be guardian of our herds,
> Leaving to fools such fine-drawn niceties,
> Their guerdon empty stores and poverty.

In the description which is given above of the probable conduct of Socrates before a court of justice we recognize the actual scene of his trial, and in the "mean and low accuser" the insignificant Meletus who appeared upon that occasion as plaintiff. The charges of impiety preferred against Socrates not only admitted of his being "dragged to prison" without any previous summons before a judge, but left it to the accuser to propose the penalty of his offence.

NOTE 43, p. 61.

Of TISANDER nothing is known. ANDRON, who is mentioned in the *Protagoras* as one of the group gathered round Hippias, is supposed to have been the father of Androtion, a disciple of the celebrated orator Isocrates. NAUSICYDES is probably the meal merchant mentioned by Xenophon as "so wealthy that he maintains not only himself and his household, but many sheep and cattle in addition, and over and above all this makes so much that he is able to perform frequent services to the state." — *Mem.* II. vii. 6.

NOTE 44, p. 67.

This peculiarity in the conversations of Socrates seems to have become a standing joke among his contemporaries. Alcibiades remarks that "he talks only about pack asses and blacksmiths and cobblers and tanners, and always appears to say the same thing in the same words." — *Symp.* 221 E. And Xenophon tells us that Critias, one of the thirty tyrants, forbade him again to mention the name of "tanner and carpenter or blacksmith; for," he adds, " I think you have worn them threadbare, so much have you talked about them."— XEN. *Mem.* I. ii., 37. It is related that Hippias, the man of "universal pretensions," on accosting him one day with the remark, " Do you mean to say, Socrates, that you are still repeating the same things which I heard you saying ages ago?" received the following answer: " Nay, Hippias, what is still more remarkable, I not only keep on saying the same things, but upon the same subjects also. Now you, I suppose, with your universal knowledge, never by any chance say twice the same things upon the same subject."— XEN. *Mem.* IV. iv. 6. See page 119, where Socrates gives it as a proof of incapacity that "we can never hold to the same opinion upon the same questions, though they be of the greatest importance."

NOTE 45, p. 68.

In some of the texts the words "the rulers than the ruled" are added here.

A little further on (lines 31–2) there is another difference of reading, the question of Callicles in respect to the temperate being in some of the MSS. answered by Socrates in the negative, thus : " How should I ? Every one knows I do not mean these," to which Callicles rejoins : " I should think not, indeed, Socrates."

NOTE 46, p. 69.

The same tone is adopted by Callicles in regard to temperance which Thrasymachus used when he spoke of justice as a " noble folly " (*Repub.* 348 D). Doubtless this attitude of pitying contempt proved a more effectual mode of warfare than any direct opposition would have been, since to many men any reputation is more enviable than that of fool.

NOTE 47, p. 71.

These lines are probably a quotation from the *Polyidus*, a lost tragedy of Euripides. The story runs that the seer Polyidus being unable to restore to life Glaucon, the son of Minos, was sentenced to be buried alive with the dead body of the child. While in the tomb, Polyidus observed a snake which, approaching the body of a dead snake, applied to it a certain herb, whereupon the creature was immediately restored to life. Following this example, Polyidus applied the herb to the child's body, when the same result ensued. The tale is emblematic of a theory of Heraclitus, as quoted by the pseudo-Plutarch.— *Consol. ad Apollonium*, 106 E. "Living and dying are all one ; the former changes into the latter, the latter again into the former." And in the *Phaedo*, Plato, following out the same idea, reasons that "if all things which have a part in life were to die, and after that remain in the condition of death and never come back to life again, it would follow of necessity that finally all things would be dead and nothing be left alive."— *Phaedo*, 72 C.

NOTE 48, p. 71.

It is of course impossible to render in English the play on the words σῶμα (body) and σῆμα (tomb), πίθος (vessel) and πιθανός (credulous), ἀνοήτους (thoughtless) and αμυήτους (initiated), Ἄιδου (Hades), and ἀειδής (invisible). The pun on σῶμα recalls a curious passage in the Cratylus (400 B-C.), where, after pointing out various other possible derivations of the word body, Socrates finally likens it to a prison-house; and in the *Phaedo* again he speaks of the unpurified soul as "compelled to survey the things that really exist, not through her own power but through the body as if through the bars of a dungeon." — *Ph.* 82 E.

The "ingenious man" was doubtless some follower of Orpheus or Pythagoras, who, after the manner of his school, made choice of ambiguous expressions in order to hide his real meaning from the uninitiated.

The "vessel perforated with holes" suggests the story of the Danaïdes who, in punishment for the murder of their bridegrooms, were condemned in Hades forever to pour water into a sieve. It is to this story that Aristotle alludes when, in speaking of the distribution, by the demagogues, of the surplus revenues of the state, he says that "to the needy such help as this is a perforated vessel indeed." — *Pol.* VI. 5.

NOTE 49, p. 73.

This bird was probably a kind of plover, which, Aristotle tells us, "appears in the night and runs off by day." — ARIST. *Hist. Anim.* IX. 11. It dwelt, as its name signifies, in clefts of rock formed by mountain torrents, and was believed to cure jaundice by catching the disease through its eyes, for which reason the bird dealers always kept it covered up, lest a cure should be effected for nothing.

NOTE 50, p. 75.

In this playful mention of the deme to which he and Callicles belong, Socrates imitates the formalities habitually used when solemn covenants were drawn up.

NOTE 51, p. 76.

Not only the rhetoricians, but even some of the so-called teachers of philosophy affected the same tone of contempt in which Callicles here speaks of dialectical arguments. Hippias, for instance, the Sophist who laid claim to universal knowledge, calls them "shavings" or "parings."

NOTE 52, p. 77.

The Eleusinian MYSTERIES were of two kinds, the lesser being in some sort a course of instruction in and preparation for the greater, which admitted the candidate into a full knowledge of the truths set forth under the symbolic form of Ceres' wanderings in search of her daughter Persephone. In popular belief, the mysteries purified men from guilt and secured them a favourable reception in the nether world; but we may well believe that to the thoughtful their value consisted in the removal of the sphere of contemplation from the world of sense to the world invisible and divine, and in the sense of personal communion with a higher power so wanting in the ordinary Greek worship. This is doubtless the meaning of

Plato when he asserts that "they who appointed the mysteries were no triflers, but were speaking with a hidden meaning when they said that he who went uninitiated and unconsecrated to the world below should wallow in mire, but he who had been purified by initiation should dwell with the gods. . . . And these," he adds, "are in my opinion none other than they who have truly loved wisdom." — *Phaedo,* 69 C.

NOTE 53, p. 77.

This saying, said to be of Empedocles, seems to have been a favourite with Plato, for we find it quoted in two other of his dialogues. — See *Philebus,* 59 E; *Laws,* 956 E.

NOTE 54, p. 78.

By this concession Callicles shows that he is not prepared to carry to all lengths the hedonism or theory of pleasure which he has been preaching. " Do you suppose," says Protarchus in the *Philebus* (13 B), "that when a man has once established the fact of pleasure being a good, he would suffer you to say that while some pleasures are goods others are evils ?" " Having pleasure I should have everything" (*Phil.* 21 B) is the confession of the true hedonist.

NOTE 55, p. 79.

Dithyrambic verse, originally composed to be sung in honour of Dionysus at vintage time, had of recent years suffered grave deterioration at the hands of Cinesias, Meles, and other "twisters of song" (Aristophanes, *Nubes.* 333), who through their "discordant lawlessness," and their ignorance of "what is lawful and just in music, conduct themselves after the manner of frenzied bacchanals and are overmastered by pleasure, . . .' falsely and ignorantly testifying of music that there is no intrinsic rightness about it, and that whether it is good or bad may be rightly determined only by the degree of pleasure which the hearer finds therein." — *Laws,* 700 D-E.

The flute, in Sparta employed for military purposes, was held in Athens as unfit for a freeman's use. The contortions of face, unavoidable in playing upon the instrument, may account in great measure for this prejudice, but a more serious objection is the declaration of Plato that "when a man suffers the music of the flute, through the ears as if through a funnel, to subdue and overcome his soul, . . . he begins to melt and waste away, until at last his spirit is melted out of him, and the sinews, as it were, of his soul are cut away, and he becomes a feeble warrior indeed." — *Repub.* 411, A–B.

Owing to the exciting effect produced by the music of the flute, it was used in such ceremonies as the mystic rites of Bacchus and the Phrygian Cybele, which demanded a religious frenzy on the part of the worshippers. In the *Crito*, Socrates compares himself to the Corybantes, the priests of Cybele, because even as the sound of the flutes resounds within them so does the echo of the voice of the Laws resound within himself, making him unable to hear aught beside. — *Crito*, 54 E.

NOTE 56, p. 80.

The likeness here spoken of between rhetoric and poetry was perhaps suggested by the style of Euripides, which was more rhetorical than that of his predecessors. But to his style only can the comparison apply, for this poet never misses a chance of introducing moral instruction, sometimes even to the point of weariness.

Although Plato in more than one instance has shown how just is his own appreciation of poetry, he habitually decries its use as profitless and even pernicious to the state. "We ourselves," he asserts, "are, to the extent of our power, poets of the best and noblest tragedy; for our whole constitution is an imitation of the best and noblest life, and this we declare to be the truest tragedy." — *Laws*, 817 B. And elsewhere he warns us of the danger of giving ourselves up, as we do in fiction, to feelings which in our own lives it is our study to repress: "We seldom take into account that in this way we get the benefit of other people's afflictions; for if we foster into strength pity for others' woes it becomes no easy matter to hold in check pity for our own woes." — *Repub.* 606 B.

From the reference to women in this passage, and from the statement that in deciding upon the most pleasurable form of entertainment, big boys would give the preference to comedy, children to puppet shows, and women to tragedy (*Laws*, 658 D), it would seem that women were admitted to at least some of the theatrical representations, although Aristophanes, in his classification of an Athenian audience (*Pax.* 50), implies that they were excluded from the comedy.

Note 57, p. 81.

But two of these four statesmen can be said to have proved themselves indifferent to the best interests of the citizens: Miltiades, the commander at Marathon, the victory which "chastened the arrogance of all Asia," and Themistocles, one of the generals at Salamis, where the Greeks, it has been said, learned not to fear the barbarians at sea, as at Marathon they had learned not to fear them on land. The great wealth and splendid abilities of Themistocles were unscrupulously used in the furtherance of his own selfish ambition, to the utter disregard of his country's imminent ruin, and the forces entrusted to Miltiades for public defence were diverted to a private enterprise destined to satisfy his greed of gain. Of the two remaining names, Cimon, the son of Miltiades, and, like Themistocles, one of the generals at Salamis, from his lavish acts of generosity, such as spreading daily an open table, distributing garments to the needy, and removing the walls from his garden that all might have free use of it, may have laid himself open to the charge of pandering to the populace, although there is no real evidence that he was actuated by any other spirit than that of genuine liberality. The accusation against Pericles was of different origin. No love of ostentatious display could be attributed to a man whose fortune was as moderate as his use of it was economical, but on the other hand the innovations sanctioned, if not instituted, by him,—the payment of salaries to officers of the state that they might not suffer pecuniary loss in the fulfilment of public duties, the free gift of entrance fees to the theatre, the adornment of Athens, which fostered the love of the beautiful, were doubtless set down by the conservative and aristocratic party to which Socrates belonged as so many specimens of the "flattering art" by which the people were cajoled into compliance with the ruler's will. And this to them was signal proof that he was lacking in true statesmanship, and hence incapable of fulfilling the highest duties of his office, even though, in virtue of a certain heaven-born instinct or inspiration akin to that of the poet, he might have power to guide his own course aright. — *Meno*, 99 C–D.

NOTE 58, p. 81.

The analogy between the body and the soul is frequently dwelt upon by Plato. True rhetoric he defines as "an art of the same kind as medicine. . . . for in the one art the essential nature of the body, as in the other that of the soul, must be thoroughly understood, if, not in a tentative and experimental manner but scientifically by means of food and medicine, you would implant health and strength in the former, and in the latter, by the use of precepts and proper training, that conviction which it is your object to bring about — even virtue." — *Phaedrus*, 270 B.

"To create health," he furthermore tells us, "is to bring the various parts of the body into a natural and reciprocal relation of command and obedience ; to create disease is to bring them into an unnatural relation of ruling and being ruled. . . . And so to implant justice is to bring all belonging to the soul into the same relation of command and obedience ; to implant injustice is to bring them into an unnatural state of ruling and being ruled." — *Repub*. 444 D.

And elsewhere he warns us how useless it is to attempt the cure of the body without that of the soul, just as the cure of the eyes is not to be attempted without the head, nor that of the head without the body; "for if the whole be not well, it is impossible that the part should be." — *Charmides*, 156 E.

NOTE 59, p. 83.

This is possibly an allusion to some old superstition that an unfinished myth aroused the anger of the gods. "Every discourse," we read in the *Phaedrus* (264 C), "should be like any living creature, having its own proper body, in order that it may neither be without head nor without feet, but may possess such middle and such extremities as are suited to each other and to the whole." And in the *Laws* (752 A) the Athenian exclaims : "I should not like to let my story go wandering about everywhere without a head, for in such condition it were an unsightly object indeed."

NOTE 60, p. 83.

EPICHARMUS, born in the island of Cos, about 540 B. C., became subsequently an inhabitant of Syracuse. Although a follower of Pythagoras in philosophy, and also, it is said, a student of medicine, his chief fame was derived from his comedies, which were probably the first ever constructed upon a regular plan. They were full of sententious maxims, which are frequently quoted by Plato.

NOTE 61, p. 85.

The words "be temperate," and "know thyself," inscribed over the temple at Delphi, must, as Plato elsewhere tells us, be intended to imply that temperance is no other than self-knowledge. — *Charmides*, 164 E.

The virtue of temperance stands for that high self-control which brings about a perfect harmony of the whole nature. We are told that by virtue of temperance, "all that is lower in a man's nature is subjected to that which is higher," and he becomes in the truest sense "master of himself." — *Rep.* 430 E–431 A. And again : "The soul is healed by certain charms, which charms are noble words; and by these temperance is implanted in the soul, and when she is once implanted and established there, it becomes easy to supply health to the head and to the whole body as well." — *Char.* 157 A. It is perhaps because temperance so well lends itself to Plato's favourite analogy of soul and body, that it stands here for what justice represents in the *Republic*—the harmony of all the faculties of the soul.

NOTE 62, p. 86.

With a love of ambiguous expressions, which seems to have been inherited from the mystics, the Platonists were wont to use in place of the ordinary salutation of "*hail*," or "*be of good cheer*," that of "*do well*," which is identical with "*fare*" or "*be well*." In beginning his third epistle, Plato (or his imitator) thus alludes to his fondness for this mode of salutation : " In writing to Dionysius to be of good cheer, have I, Plato, hit upon the best mode of greeting ? Or is not my usual one of *do well* preferable, with which it is my custom to greet my friends ? "

NOTE 63, p. 87.

The phrase " never-ending torment" is an allusion like that on page 71, to the Danaïdes and their sieves. A similar idea is found in the description of the unphilosophic soul which "gives herself up again to pleasures and pains, thus fettering herself anew and undertaking a hopeless and futile task; weaving, as it were, the endless web of Penelope, only with a contrary design." — *Phaed.* 84 A.

NOTE 64, p. 87.

The study of arithmetic was forbidden by Lycurgus at Sparta, because the computation of numbers was supposed to be levelling and democratic in its tendency. Geometry, on the other hand, which deals with relative proportions, was encouraged as the embodiment of that conservative principle of order which in the system of Empedocles is represented by friendship and love, while discord and dissension stand for the changeful and destructive in the universe. " Let no one who is ignorant of geometry enter under my roof " is said to have been the inscription which Plato caused to be inscribed over the entrance to the Academy.

This principle of geometrical order and equality, which "to the greater apportions more, to the inferior less, bestowing upon each one that measure which befits him (*Laws* 757 A-

C), is the same which is called by Aristotle "distributive justice" (*Nic. Eth.* V. 7, p. 1131 b), and which, being recognized by the Pythagoreans as the source of "temperance" in the social state and of harmony in the realm of nature, suggested to them the name of Cosmos or order as that most truly descriptive of the universe.

NOTE 65, p. 91.

This recalls a passage in Xenophon's *Apology* (28), where Apollodorus exclaims: "To me, Socrates, the hardest part is to see you suffering death without just cause." To which Socrates, stroking his hair, replied: "Would you, then, dearest Apollodorus, prefer to see me suffer death for just cause?"

"To the unregenerate Prometheus Vinctus of a man," says Carlyle, "it is ever the bitterest aggravation of his wretchedness that he is conscious of virtue, that he feels himself the victim not of suffering only, but of injustice." — *Sartor Resartus*, chap. vii.

NOTE 66, p. 92.

The OBOLE or OBOLUS was equal to about three cents of our money.

NOTE 67, p. 93.

Compare with *Crito*, 47 D-E: "Would life be worth living with a miserable corrupt body?... or would it be worth living if that part of us were corrupt which injustice degrades and justice benefits?" And with the *Repub.* 445 B: "If it is impossible to live when the bodily constitution is corrupted, even though we have food and drink of every variety and all manner of riches and power, how can it be possible to live when the very principle by which we live is corrupted, even though we be at liberty to do anything we please, save the one thing alone whereby we may escape evil and injustice and attain justice and virtue?"

"While they promise them liberty, they themselves are the servants of corruption, for of whom a man is overcome, of the same is he brought in bondage." — 2 *Peter* ii. 19.

Note 68, p. 95.

"It is not mere living which should be valued above everything else, but living a good life," were the words of Socrates on being warned of his approaching end (*Crito*, 48 B), and his last exhortation to his friends was to be " of good courage and await the journey to the world below, ready to set forth whenever the voice of fate shall call." —*Phaed.* 115 A.

Note 69, p. 95.

An allusion to the story that certain witches of Thessaly, where the black arts were much practised, took advantage of the knowledge bestowed upon them by Hecate, the goddess of the moon, and drew that planet down from heaven, for which presumption they were punished by the indignant goddess with the loss of their eyes and feet, or, as sometimes interpreted, of their children. The warning is intended for the ambitious, who in the struggle for political dignities too often make shipwreck of their own true dignity and manhood.

Note 70, p. 97.

As the ceramic art was at this time in its perfection at Athens, the trade of potter was naturally taken as an illustration of manual dexterity; the obvious application being that public office, like the fashioning of large wine jars, is not to be entered upon, until, by practice upon a more modest scale, the necessary ability has been attained.

Note 71, p. 98.

The Lacedaemonians or Spartans were given this sobriquet on account of the frequent mutilation of their ears resulting from their pugilistic exercises. In the *Protagoras* (342 B), certain persons are spoken of as " going about with their ears bruised in imitation of the Lacedaemonians."

The aristocratic tendencies of Socrates, which led to his being accused of an excessive partiality for Sparta, caused him to regard it as an experiment no less farcical than it was imprudent to invest the uneducated masses with either political or judicial power. Aristophanes turns the then existing system into ridicule, describing how, for the price of three oboli, the citizens sit all day long in the courts under the delusion that they are conducting public affairs, when in reality they have no more power than so many children in leading strings.—*Wasps*, 666-695.

The charge made against Pericles has its foundation in the newly instituted custom already mentioned (Note 56), of paying the soldiers, judges, and assemblymen that they might not, from the suspension of their various callings, suffer loss in their fulfilment of public duties.

Note 72, p. 99.

In the second year of the Peloponnesian war, the Athenians, decimated by the plague and crippled by reverses, accused Pericles, their general in chief, of having brought these evils upon them. That there was any question of his being condemned to death is probably an exaggeration, although he was certainly not reëlected general, and was sentenced to pay a heavy fine. The sentence, however, was shortly afterwards revoked, and Pericles was reinstated, with a formal expression of regret for the injustice done him.

The passage which follows is almost identical with one in the *Memorabilia*, where Socrates, in speaking of the evil influence exerted by the thirty tyrants, remarks that "it were an amazing thing if a man who had caused the herd of which he was keeper to deteriorate and become worse oxen did not acknowledge himself to be a bad oxherd; but still more amazing if a man who, acting as overseer of a city, had caused the citizens to deteriorate and become worse men, did not feel shame and regard himself as a bad overseer of the city."— XEN. *Mem.* I. 2, 32.

Note 73, p. 100.

Although these words are not a direct quotation, their sense is expressed in two passages in the *Odyssey*:—

"What men are here — wild, savage, and unjust,
Or hospitable, and who hold the gods
In reverence?"

— vi., 120.

"Whether ill-mannered, savage, and unjust,
Or kind to guests and reverent towards the gods."

— ix., 175. [Bryant's translation.

NOTE 74, p. 100.

Ostracism, so called from the tile (ὄστρακον) on which the name of the person to be condemned was written, seems to have been regarded less as a punishment than as a preventive measure for averting future danger and possible bloodshed to the state, by the precautionary removal of some citizen whose wealth or position might enable him to usurp an undue share of power. This measure to be carried into effect required first the consent of the people in a regular assembly, after which a public meeting was convened in the agora, when each voter wrote upon a tile the name of the citizen he wished to have removed. Whoever received the largest number of votes, provided the number was not under six thousand, was compelled to leave Attica for a period of ten years, though he might be recalled at any time by a vote of the people, as in the case of Cimon, who was recalled at the instance of his rival, Pericles.

Banishment was a much severer punishment, and attended with disgrace, but the property of the condemned was not necessarily confiscated, and even when the offence had been murder, the ban was sometimes removed on payment of a penalty.

The "pit" was a "place like a well," said to have hooks or spikes in the sides and at the bottom, into which condemned criminals were thrown, in earlier days probably while yet alive, but in later times only after death.

Although it is only from a one-sided point of view that the three men here mentioned can be classed in the same category, advantage is taken of a certain similarity of outward circumstance to name them collectively as examples of bad management no less than of bad statesmanship. For they had failed not only to raise the moral character of the citizens but also to secure their own chief aim — the approval and confidence of those whom they sought to flatter; and thus, while forfeiting the approval of their own conscience, they shared equally with the honest man all the penalties of unpopularity.

NOTE 75, p. 103.

THEARION is mentioned by more than one of the comic poets as the fashionable baker of Athens.

MITHAECUS of Sicily, a country which in culinary matters was to Greece what France is to the rest of Europe, was said to be as great a cook as Phidias was a sculptor, and was much appreciated in all the Greek cities, with the exception of Sparta, where it was a point of discipline to discourage his profession. To him is attributed the honour of having written the first cookery book ever made.

The skill of SARAMBUS in mixing wines, an important part of the office of wine-seller, was, according to a comic poet (POSIDIPPUS, *Fr. Inc.* iii.), one of Plataea's few boasts.

NOTE 76, p. 104.

The blame of Athens' decline was laid in great part upon ALCIBIADES, by whose advice the ill-fated Sicilian expedition had been undertaken.

NOTE 77, p. 107.

The MYSIANS, a people of Asia Minor, were, together with the Carians, regarded as so inferior a race that their name was used as an epithet of lowest opprobrium.

NOTE 78, p. 110.

From the Apology of Socrates we learn that the charges which he is here supposed to foretell were not wholly unprovoked. His simile of the gadfly (*Ap.* 30 E) is no inapt representation of the manner in which his searching and persistent investigation must have acted upon the superficial hearer, to whom doubtless it appeared that "like the torpedo fish . . . which torpifies all who come within its touch," he did "nothing but bewilder himself and other people" (*Meno*, 80 A), and was "a most eccentric creature, who drove men to their wits' end." — *Theactetus*, 149 A.

They, on the other hand, who yielded themselves to him "as to a physician," failed not to learn that by this process of cross examination the mind, being purged of all prejudices and preconceived notions (*Soph*. 230 D), was for the first time opened to receive the truth.

NOTE 79, p. 111.

"The hard thing," so Socrates addresses his judges after he has received sentence of condemnation, "is to escape not death but evil, for that runs faster than death. — *Ap*. 39 A.

"Strange were it," he says again, "if through fear of death or any other evil, I were to desert my post. . . . For no one knows what death is, or whether it may not be the greatest of all goods to men . . . but that it is wicked and disgraceful to do injustice, and to disobey a superior, whether God or man, this I do know. Those evils, therefore, which I know to be evils, not those things which for aught I know may be blessings, will I fear and flee from." — *Ap*. 29 C.

But more triumphant is the strain where Socrates welcomes death, the "best friend of man" (*Laws*, 828 D), even as do the swans, who "when they perceive that death is near sing much more fully and freely than they have sung all their life before out of joy that they are about to go and dwell with the god whose servants they are . . . and, because they can look into the unseen world, rejoice on that day more than upon any other day of their life." — *Phaed.* 85 A, B.

NOTE 80, p. 111.

The passage is from the *Iliad* (15, 187 fol.), where Poseidon says: —

> "We were three brothers, all of Rhaea born
> To Saturn; Jove and I, and Pluto third

> Who o'er the nether regions holds his sway.
> Threefold was our partition; each obtained
> His meed of honours due; the hoary Sea
> By lot my habitation was assigned;
> The realms of Darkness fell to Pluto's share;
> Broad Heaven amid the sky and clouds to Jove,
> But Earth and high Olympus are to all
> A common heritage."
> — [Lord Derby's translation.

The HAPPY or BLESSED ISLES are the same as the Elysian Fields, which Homer places on the western border of the earth, "where the sun goes down," while Hesiod speaks of them as in the ocean, and later poets again as underneath the earth. In the time of Homer these islands were believed to be the abode only of favoured heroes, who were transported thither without dying, but at this period they were thought of as inhabited by all good men after death. In the same way, Tartarus, originally supposed to be the prison-house of the Titans only, had come to be regarded as the place of punishment for all mortals.

NOTE 81, p. 112.

PROMETHEUS, having endowed men with the gift of foreknowledge, had also power to take it away and substitute for it hope. In the words of Æschylus : —

Prom. "I made men cease from contemplating death."
Chorus. "What medicine didst thou find for that disease?"
Prom. "Blind hopes I gave to live and dwell with them."
— *Prometheus*, vv. 247 seq. [Plumptre's translation.

NOTE 82, p. 113.

At this day only two continents, EUROPE and ASIA, were recognised. MINOS and RHADAMANTHUS, the representatives of Asia, were born in Crete, whence it must be inferred that this island was regarded as belonging not to Europe but to Asia. Minos, the fabled king and law-giver of Crete, who exacted from Athens the yearly sacrifice to the Minotaur of fourteen youths and maidens, is thus spoken of in the *Odyssey*: —

> " Then I beheld the illustrious son of Zeus,
> Minos, a golden sceptre in his hand,

> Sitting to judge the dead who round the king
> Pleaded their cause."
>
> — *Od.* xi., 707. [Bryant's translation.

The "meadow at the three cross-roads" recalls —

> "the fields of asphodel where dwelt
> The souls, the bodiless forms of those who die."
>
> — *Od.* xxiv., 13.

In popular superstition the meeting of three cross-roads was held to be peculiarly favourable for communication with the nether world.

NOTE 83, p. 113.

"For is not dying to have the soul and body released one from the other, so that each exists by itself? Is death anything else than this?" — *Phaed.* 64 C.

NOTE 84, p. 113.

To be closely cropped was regarded in Athens as a badge of slavery, while flowing hair on the other hand was worn only by fops. It was customary for boys to wear their hair long until they were admitted to the rights of citizenship, when it was cut off and dedicated to some deity, generally a river god, although a visit was sometimes made to Delphi for the express object of consecrating this as an offering to Apollo. Upon reaching manhood, they allowed their hair to grow again. Thucydides (I, 6) speaks of the golden clasps, in the shape of grasshoppers, wherewith the Athenians, in the old times before the Persian wars, were accustomed to fasten their hair in a knot at the top or back of the head.

NOTE 85, p. 114.

"Happy he," Carlyle exclaims, "who can look through the clothes of a man into the man himself and discern if may be in this or the other dread potentate, a more or less incompetent digestive apparatus; yet also an inscrutable mystery in the meanest tinker that sees with eyes!" — *Sartor Resartus*, Book I, chap. ix.

NOTE 86, p. 115.

The early Fathers of the Church held the teachings of the divine Plato in scarcely less reverence than those of the inspired writers, and it is very probable that the theological conception of Purgatory, so foreign to Hebrew thought, was evolved from the description of the intermediate state contained in this myth and in similar passages.

According to the view of Socrates that evil is committed through want of understanding, punishment was regarded by him not as retributive, but as corrective, if not to the sinner himself at least to his fellow-men. "A man is not punished on account of his having sinned, for what has been done can never be undone, but in order that in the time to come he and all who behold him may perfectly hate injustice, or desist in great measure from the practice of it."— *Laws*, 934 A.

NOTE 87, p. 116.

In the myth descriptive of the after life, contained in the tenth book of the *Republic*, we read that of the hopelessly lost "the greater part had been in life despots," and accordingly chief among the group figures Ardiaeus, the tyrant king of Pamphylia.— *Repub.* 615 E. So Fra Angelico and other mediæval painters, in their pictures of the Last Judgment, were wont to place kings and potentates in the foremost rank of those condemned to eternal punishment.

Plato maintained also that great natural endowments are fraught with scarcely less danger to their owner than is high position. "Do not the greatest crimes," he exclaims, "and depravity the most unalloyed, proceed, not from a worthless nature, but rather from the exuberance of one which its training has spoiled; and is it not true that a weak nature is capable neither of great good nor of great evil?"— *Repub.* 491 E.

NOTE 88, p. 116.

TANTALUS, the ancestor of the race of Pelops and supposed to have been a king of Phrygia, was, in punishment for having divulged a secret of the gods, condemned to suffer the extremes of hunger and thirst, while powerless to reach the water and food by which he was surrounded.

> "And next I looked on Tantalus, a prey
> To grievous torments, standing in a lake
> That reached his chin. Though painfully athirst,
> He could not drink; as often as he bowed
> His aged head to take into his lips
> The water, it was drawn away, and sank
> Into the earth, and the dark soil appeared
> Around his feet; a god had dried it up."
>
> — *Od.* xi., 582.

SISYPHUS, the reputed founder of Corinth, was sentenced, for his deceit and avarice, to roll forever up hill a huge marble block, which had no sooner reached the top than it rolled down again.

> "Then I beheld the shade of Sisyphus
> Amid his sufferings. With both hands he rolled
> A huge stone up a hill. To force it up
> He leaned against the mass with hands and feet;
> But, ere it crossed the summit of the hill,
> A power was felt that sent it rolling back,
> And downward plunged the unmanageable rock
> Before him to the plain. Again he toiled
> To heave it upward, while the sweat in streams
> Ran down his limbs, and dust begrimed his brow."
>
> — *Od.* xi., 593.

The giant TITYUS was sent to Tartarus in punishment for an offence against Leto (Latona).

> "And Tityus there I saw, — the mighty earth
> His mother, overspreading, as he lay,
> Nine acres, with two vultures at his side,
> That, plucking at his liver, plunged their beaks
> Into the flesh; nor did his hands avail
> To drive them off."
>
> — *Od.* xi., 576. [Bryant's translation.

In the second book of the *Iliad* we read of the council of war where THERSITES, the "ugliest man who came to Troy," meets with condign punishment at the hands of Odysseus for his craven advice to abandon the siege.

Note 89, p. 117.

The omission of ARISTIDES the Just from the list of those whose statesmanship was commended by Callicles is in itself a proof of his absolute freedom from selfish ambition. He it was who before the battle of Marathon persuaded the generals, his colleagues, to relinquish each his day of command to Miltiades, by which sacrifice success was insured. When his advice was asked concerning the proposal of Themistocles to set fire to the fleet of the Greek allies and thus secure to Athens the sovereignty of the sea, he declared to the people that nothing could be more advantageous but nothing more unjust, and thus shamed them into abandoning the scheme. Ostracised through the intrigues of his rival, Themistocles, his integrity and disinterestedness were soon found to be indispensable to the state, and he was recalled to take an active part in the Persian war. So faithful and devoted was he in the discharge of all the public trusts committed to him that his private interests were neglected, and such was his poverty that at his death he was buried at public cost.

Note 90, p. 117.

"Then I beheld the illustrious son of Zeus,
Minos, a golden sceptre in his hand,
Sitting to judge the dead, who round the king
Pleaded their causes."

— *Od.* ix., 568–570.

A passage in Homer (*Iliad*, ii. 101 fol.), which recounts the descent of this badge of office in unbroken line from the ancestors of Agamemnon, one of the sceptred kings, shows that it was handed down from father to son as the outward symbol of royalty as it was also of authority, whether vested in king, judge, herald, seer, or priest.

Note 91, p. 118.

Here Socrates turns the tables upon Callicles, by repeating for his benefit the same warning which the latter had previously addressed to him (pages 58, 59).

There is a similar passage in *Theactetus*, where the philosopher who, quite unused to "refuting in rhetorical fashion" (*Gorg.* 471 E), has heretofore cut a sorry figure in the law courts, confronts the lawyer with weighty questions concerning justice and injustice, happiness and misery, and how these may be gained or avoided. And then, we are told, it is the turn of the "sharp little pettifogging mind" to become "dizzy and sore bewildered and dismayed," and to "stammer out broken words" and make himself an object of ridicule in the eyes of all "who have not the spirit of a slave." — *Theact.* 175 D.

NOTE 92, p. 119.

An allusion to line 592 in Æschylus's tragedy of the *Seven against Thebes*, which runs thus: "Best to *be* not *seem* he makes his life's pursuit." As proof of the estimation in which Aristides was held, the story is told that on the first representation of the play, the substitution of *just* for *best* in this line was the signal for every eye to be turned upon "Aristides the Just."

NOTES ON THE REPUBLIC.

NOTE 93, p. 122.

We may suppose this screen to have been a sort of bench which hid from the audience the contrivances necessary for tricks of legerdemain, or it may be that the "jugglers" were marionette players who, like the modern showman in Punch and Judy, moved their puppets from behind the screen where they were themselves concealed.

NOTE 94, p. 126.

These words are taken from the account given by Odysseus of his descent into Hades, where the ghost of Achilles says:—

"I would be
A labourer on earth, and serve for hire
Some man of mean estate who makes scant cheer
Rather than reign o'er all who have gone down
To death."
—*Od.* xi. 489–90. [Bryant's translation.

NOTE 95, p. 127.

This refers to the passage in the preceding book, where the sun is called the lord of light and the soul is compared to the eye. "When it is stayed upon that on which truth and being shine, it thinks and apprehends and beams with intelligence; but when it is turned to the darkness, it is dim-sighted and conjectures only, and changes its mind backwards and forwards, and is like to one in whom there is no intelligence."— *Repub.* 508 D.

NOTE 96, p. 128.

We are reminded here of Callicles's description of the dazed appearance which Socrates would present in a court of law, and of Socrates's own account of what would be his experience if brought before a court of little boys on a charge preferred by a pastry cook. — *Gorgias*, 486 B; 521 E; see also Note 91.

NOTE 97, p. 129.

O men forever striving, but in vain,
Why is it that a thousand arts you teach,
But one nor know nor even seek to know, —
To make him think in whom there is no mind!
— EURIPIDES, *Hippolytus*, 916 seqq.

NOTE 98, p. 130.

In the tenth book of the *Republic* Glaucon is bidden contemplate the human soul, not as she is now, corrupted through contact with the body, but such as she might become if she were "brought safely out of the sea wherein at the present she lies sunk, having shaken off the shells and pebbles, wild masses of earthy and stony substance, which, by reason of her enjoyment upon earth of the so-called good things of life, cling close about her." — *Repub.* 611 E.

NOTE 99, p. 133.

Compare Crito (50-2), where the Laws, after enumerating all the benefits that Socrates has received from them since his birth, exhort him not to break the covenant which, by voluntarily accepting their guardianship, he made with them to perform whatever they might command.

The abstinence from the turmoil of public life which Socrates elsewhere enjoins upon the philosopher may seem in direct contradiction with these exhortations to the "best endowed natures" to take part in it, just as the admonitions of that "divine voice" which always stands in the way of his having anything to do with public affairs (*Apol.* 31 E), may appear to gainsay the declaration, expressed almost in the same breath, that he is continually busying himself with the affairs of other men. — *Apol.* 31 B.

But the two are in reality not at variance ; for although it is right that the philosophic soul, renouncing worldly honours and withdrawing herself from all that appertains to the body, should in a certain sense dwell apart in the calm which she has prepared for herself (*Phaed.* 84 A), none the less does the true philosopher, even though not himself engaging in public affairs, make it his study to render others capable of engaging in them (XEN. *Mem.* I. 6, 15), reflecting that he whose training has best fitted him to do this service to the State is "as under stress of necessity" to fulfil it.

EPOCHS OF ANCIENT HISTORY.

A SERIES OF BOOKS NARRATING THE HISTORY OF GREECE AND ROME, AND OF THEIR RELATIONS TO OTHER COUNTRIES AT SUCCESSIVE EPOCHS.

Edited by

Rev. G. W. Cox and CHARLES SANKEY, M.A.

Eleven volumes, 16mo, with 41 Maps and Plans.
Sold separately. Price per vol., $1.00.
The Set, Roxburgh style, gilt top, in box, $11.00.

TROY—ITS LEGEND, HISTORY, AND LITERATURE. By S. G. W. BENJAMIN.

THE GREEKS AND THE PERSIANS. By the Rev. G. W. Cox.

THE ATHENIAN EMPIRE—From the Flight of Xerxes to the Fall of Athens. By the Rev. G. W. Cox.

THE SPARTAN AND THEBAN SUPREMACIES. By CHARLES SANKEY, M.A.

THE MACEDONIAN EMPIRE—Its Rise and Culmination to the Death of Alexander the Great. By A. M. CURTEIS, M.A.

The five volumes above give a connected and complete history of Greece from the earliest times to the death of Alexander.

EARLY ROME—From the Foundation of the City to its Destruction by the Gauls. By W. IHNE, Ph.D.

ROME AND CARTHAGE—The Punic Wars. By R. BOSWORTH SMITH, M.A.

THE GRACCHI, MARIUS, AND SULLA. By A. H. BEESLY, M.A.

THE ROMAN TRIUMVIRATES. By the Very Rev. CHARLES MERIVALE, D.D.

THE EARLY EMPIRE—From the Assassination of Julius Cæsar to the Assassination of Domitian. By the Rev. W. WOLFE CAPES, M.A.

THE AGE OF THE ANTONINES—the Roman Empire of the Second Century. By the Rev. W. WOLFE CAPES, M.A.

The six volumes above give the History of Rome from the founding of the City to the death of Marcus Amelius Antoninus.

EPOCHS OF HISTORY.

"A Series of concise and carefully prepared volumes on special eras of history. Each is devoted to a group of events of such importance as to entitle it to be regarded as an epoch. Each is also complete in itself, and has no especial connection with the other members of the series. The works are all written by authors selected by the editor on account of some especial qualifications for a portrayal of the period they respectively describe. The volumes form an excellent collection, especially adapted to the wants of a general reader."—*CHARLES KENDALL ADAMS, President of Cornell University.*

"The 'Epochs of History' seem to me to have been prepared with knowledge and artistic skill to meet the wants of a large number of readers. To the young they furnish an outline or compendium which may serve as an introduction to more extended study. To those who are older they present a convenient sketch of the heads of the knowledge which they have already acquired. The outlines are by no means destitute of spirit, and may be used with great profit for family reading, and in select classes or reading clubs."—*NOAH PORTER, President of Yale College.*

"It appears to me that the idea of Morris in his Epochs is strictly in harmony with the philosophy of history—namely, that great movements should be treated not according to narrow geographical and national limits and distinction, but universally, according to their place in the general life of the world. The historical Maps and the copious Indices are welcome additions to the volumes."—*Bishop JOHN F. HURST, Ex-President of Drew Theological Seminary.*

"The volumes contain the ripe results of the studies of men who are authorities in their respective fields."—*The Nation.*

"To be appreciated they must be read in their entirety; and we do no more than simple justice in commending them earnestly to the favor of the studious public."—*The New York World.*

The great success of the series is the best proof of its general popularity, and the excellence of the various volumes is further attested by their having been adopted as text-books in many of our leading educational institutions, including Harvard, Cornell, Wesleyan, Vermont, and Syracuse Universities; Yale, Princeton, Amherst, Dartmouth, Williams, Union, and Smith Colleges; and many other colleges, academies, normal and high schools.

SOCRATES: A Translation of the Apology, Crito, and parts of the Phædo of Plato, containing the Defence of Socrates at his Trial, his Conversations in Prison, with his Thoughts on the Future Life, and an Account of his Death. With an Introduction by Professor W. W. GOODWIN, of Harvard College. 12mo, cloth, $1.00; paper, 50 cents.

A DAY IN ATHENS WITH SOCRATES:
Translations from the Protagoras and the Republic of Plato. Being conversations between Socrates and other Greeks on Virtue and Justice. 12mo, cloth, $1.00; paper, 50 cents.

These exquisite translations, by an unknown hand, of some of Plato's immortal masterpieces have been pronounced by those best qualified to judge, to be the best English versions that have ever been made of the dialogues and speculations of the greatest philosopher of all times in a form for popular reading.

The first of the volumes is intended to present the personal character and moral position of Socrates, together with Plato's own speculations. The companion volume has for its object to give a vivid picture, not so much of Plato's philosophy as of the distinctive characteristics of the age in which he lived, and to enable the reader to enter into the every-day scenes of Athenian life, and to become, as it were, an actual participator in the action.

These books are especially to be commended for the use of school libraries and reading circles. No better examples exist of the popularization of high class literature that is a feature of our times.

THE DIALOGUES OF PLATO
Translated into English, with Analysis and Introductions
By B. JOWETT, M.A.
MASTER OF BALLIOL COLLEGE, OXFORD, AND REGIUS PROFESSOR OF GREEK

A new and cheaper edition. Four vols., crown 8vo, $8.00 per set, in cloth

From the NEW YORK TRIBUNE.

"The present work of Professor Jowett will be welcomed with profound interest, as the only adequate endeavor to transport the most precious monument of Grecian thought among the familiar treasures of English literature. The noble reputation of Professor Jowett, both as a thinker and a scholar, it may be premised, however, is a valid guaranty for the excellence of his performance. He is known as one of the most hard-working students of the English universities, in the departments of philology and criticism, whose exemplary diligence is fully equalled by his singular acuteness of penetration, his clear and temperate judgment, and his rare and absolute fidelity to the interests of truth."

PLATO'S BEST THOUGHTS
As compiled from Professor Jowett's Translation of the Dialogues of Plato
By REV. C H. A. BULKLEY

A new edition. One vol., crown 8vo, price reduced to $1.50

From THE EVANGELIST.

"This volume makes the best things in Plato accessible and available and its index gives it the character of a dictionary."

MANUAL OF MYTHOLOGY

For the Use of Schools, Art Students, and General Readers

FOUNDED ON THE WORKS OF PETISCUS, PRELLER, AND WELCKER

By ALEXANDER S. MURRAY

DEPARTMENT OF GREEK AND ROMAN ANTIQUITIES, BRITISH MUSEUM

With 45 Plates on tinted paper, representing more than 90 Mythological Subjects. Reprinted from the Second Revised London Edition

One vol., crown 8vo, ... $2.25

There was long needed a compact, manageable Manual of Mythology, which should be a guide to the Art student and the general reader, and at the same time answer the purposes of a school text-book. This volume which was prepared by the Director of the Department of Greek and Roman Antiquities in the British Museum, upon the basis of the works of Petiscus, Preller, and Welcker, had so extensive a sale in the English edition, as to prove that it precisely supplied this want. This American edition is reprinted from the latest English edition, and contains all the illustrations of the latter, *while the chapter upon Eastern Mythology has been carefully revised by Prof. W. D. Whitney, of Yale College.*

THE HISTORY OF ROME

From the Earliest Time to the Period of its Decline

By DR. THEODOR MOMMSEN

Translated, with the author's sanction and additions, by the REV. W. P. DICKSON, Regius Professor of Biblical Criticism in the University of Glasgow, late Classical Examiner of the University of St. Andrews. With an Introduction by DR. LEONHARD SCHMITZ, and a copious Index of the whole four volumes, prepared especially for this edition.

REPRINTED FROM THE REVISED LONDON EDITION

Four vols., crown 8vo, gilt top, price per set, . . . $8.00

"A work of the very highest merit; its learning is exact and profound; its narrative full of genius and skill; its descriptions of men are admirably vivid. We wish to place on record our opinion that Dr. Mommsen's is by far the best history of the Decline and Fall of the Roman Commonwealth."—*London Times.*

THE HISTORY OF GREECE

By PROF. DR. ERNST CURTIUS

Translated by ADOLPHUS WILLIAM WARD, M.A., Fellow of St. Peter's College, Cambridge, Prof. of History in Owen's College, Manchester.

UNIFORM WITH MOMMSEN'S HISTORY OF ROME

Five vols., crown 8vo, gilt top, price per set, . . $10.00

"We cannot express our opinion of Dr. Curtius's book better than by saying that it may be fitly ranked with Theodor Mommsen's great work."—*London Spectator.*

"The History of Greece is treated by Dr. Curtius so broadly and freely in the spirit of the nineteenth century, that it becomes in his hands one of the worthiest and most instructive branches of study for all who desire something more than a knowledge of isolated facts for their education. This translation ought to become a regular part of the accepted course of reading for young men at college, and for all who are in training for the free political life of our country."—*N. Y. Evening Post.*

CHARLES SCRIBNER'S SONS, PUBLISHERS,

743 and 745 Broadway, New York.

www.ingramcontent.com/pod-product-compliance
Lightning Source LLC
Chambersburg PA
CBHW020915230426
43666CB00008B/1458